Christian Caregiving—a Way of Life

LEADER'S GUIDE

What Pastors and Lay Leaders Are Saying:

"I had been looking for a resource that would help people understand their faith as a living force that shapes their everyday lives. This course does that and more!"

"There were many 'aha' moments in the class as people saw Christian caregiving in a whole new light."

"Since we began offering this course, there's been a new atmosphere in our congregation. There's more warmth and more smiles."

"This course has ignited a new spirit of community and cooperation in our congregation."

"I never had so much fun teaching a class!"

"We now offer this class to all new members. Not only does it help them grow in their life of faith, but it's a great way to get to know others."

Christian Caregiving—a Way of Life
LEADER'S GUIDE

What Course Participants Are Saying:

"Because of *Christian Caregiving—a Way of Life,* I feel much more confident about caring for others in a way that reflects who I am as a Christian."

"I grew tremendously going through this course. I am much more sensitive and responsive to those in need."

"I am amazed that I'm no longer nervous about praying with others."

"Biblical stories and passages about caregiving are now more important to me."

"My relationship with God has grown deeper through this course."

"I'm moving caregiving to the front line of my life!"

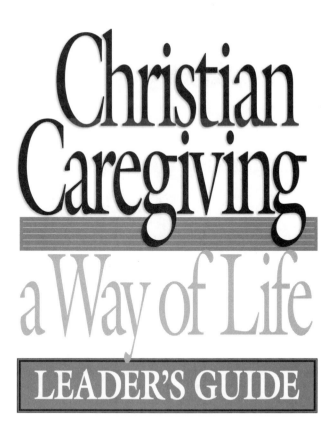

Christian Caregiving

a Way of Life

LEADER'S GUIDE

ALSO BY KENNETH C. HAUGK

ALSO BY WILLIAM J. McKAY

- *Me, an Evangelist? Every Christian's Guide to Caring Evangelism*
- *Caring Evangelism: How to Live and Share Christ's Love*
    Leader's Guide
    Administrative Handbook
    Participant Manual
- *Nuts & Bolts Issues for Small Group Leaders*
- *Beginnings*
    Group Leader Guide
    Group Member Guide
- *Spiritual Growth through Spiritual Gifts*
    Group Leader Guide
    Group Member Manual

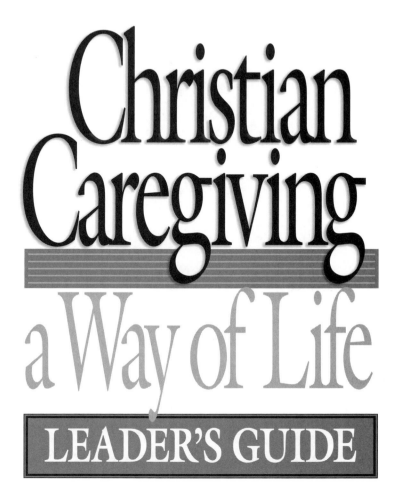

Christian Caregiving
a Way of Life
LEADER'S GUIDE

Kenneth C. Haugk
William J. McKay

STEPHEN MINISTRIES • St. Louis, Missouri

Christian Caregiving—a Way of Life Leader's Guide

ISBN: 978-1-930445-31-4

Library of Congress Control Number: 2013933639

Printed in the U.S.A.

13

To all those who seek to live the love they have received from Jesus.

A new command I give you: Love one another.
As I have loved you, so you must love one another.
John 13:34

CONTENTS

FOREWORD

You are in for a real serendipity (one surprise after another) when you lead others in a journey through Kenneth Haugk's book, *Christian Caregiving—a Way of Life*, using this leader's guide. It was a happy surprise for me to see the quality of this approach to more distinctively Christian caring and relating. I find the possibilities contained in this resource to be exciting and desperately needed.

This is not a book that you read as much as a tool to enable serendipitous encounters between people. I don't want to spoil your surprise, but here's a sneak preview of what to expect.

Surprise! The materials are so tightly structured and well done that you find yourself leading a group in ways you never thought possible. The materials enable the leader to be confident and competent, even if he or she has had little or no professional leadership training.

Happy surprise! Together your group encounters God's calling in your lives and you find yourselves discovering positive, concrete ways to respond.

Very happy surprise! Your group will grow in care for each other. They will live out Christian caregiving with each other and find themselves experiencing a richness of community and care they have never known before.

It really shouldn't come as any surprise that these materials are of such high quality. Dr. Haugk and the Stephen Ministries organization are unquestionably the finest combination in the church today when it comes to equipping the laity for ministry. While the *Christian Caregiving—a Way of Life Leader's Guide* is different from the Stephen Series, it is done with the same refreshing combination of Christian understanding, healthy psychology, and care-full attention to detail that have made the Stephen Series such a marvelous gift to the church.

If you are someone who believes that God has given to the church the responsibility to "equip the saints for the work of ministry," I commend this volume to you. It facilitates a marvelous experience . . . and who knows what surprises it may lead to.

So here's to Christian Caregiving! Here's to Ken Haugk and Bill McKay! Here's to Stephen Ministries! Here's to this invaluable resource! Here's to the happy surprises God has in store for you as you journey with others toward the future!

LYMAN COLEMAN
Serendipity House

A PERSONAL WORD FROM THE AUTHORS

Books share with sermons the risk of falling into and out of a person's life as isolated events unless there is some immediate call to action. How many times have you read a book and shelved it, saying, "There's some great stuff in there, and some day I'm going to do that." But do you? The material in *Christian Caregiving—a Way of Life* speaks for itself, and we are convinced that you will be compelled to go beyond just reading the text. You'll be itching to "do something."

We want that itch scratched. We want the content of *Christian Caregiving—a Way of Life* underscored and extended into your life and experiences. The most obvious way to do this was to construct a leader's guide enabling you to experience holistically the contents of the book. The infectious enthusiasm you will glean from others engaged in the same process of learning and doing will only enhance the impact of the material in *Christian Caregiving—a Way of Life*.

But why such great concern for the impact of a book? Caught up in the press of daily activities, why should anyone take the time for an intensive study of this book? There is a tapestry of reasons:

The Crucial Importance of the Content

The purpose of *Christian Caregiving—a Way of Life* is to equip the reader for a distinctively Christian lifestyle of caring and relating. The major obstacle we Christians seem to have in reaching this end is that of an "identity crisis." We may be eager to be "distinctively Christian," but what is that? By letting you experience who you are and what you can do, the book addresses this crucial need.

Distinctively Christian caring and relating is not optional or even merely desirable for the follower of Jesus. It is a necessity. Imagine a fish trying to live outside of its native environment. It would be unthinkable. The "native environment" of the Christian is in the world of caring and relating. It is imperative for Christians to recognize this reality and act congruently with it. Yet, so many Christians fail to be distinctively Christian in their caring and relating. *Christian Caregiving—a Way of Life* directly confronts this situation. It not only strives to acquaint you with your natural environment, but instills a love for it. *Christian Caregiving—a Way of Life* offers concrete steps to take so that you are moved to a deeper understanding of your life activities and your identity as a Christian.

"Who Am I, Anyway?"

One of the important questions Christians continue to ask is, "Who am I as a Christian, anyway?" It is often asked with overtones of puzzled bewilderment and occasional self-depreciation. Answers abound, but you still might find yourself musing, "Yes, but who am I . . . really?"

From the secular world, Christians are confronted by every imaginable kind of resource, philosophy, methodology, and approach to life. These are by no means all bad; many are quite good. It is just that the distinctively Christian consciousness can all too easily be lost in the shuffle. This leader's guide remedies that with a concerted effort to raise Christian consciousness and promote Christian practice.

None of us wants merely to be told who we are; we want to *experience* it and *do* it. The combination of reading this book and participating in the group experiences in this leader's guide will do much to help you in your Christian self-identity process.

An Experience in Christian Community

The answer to the "Who-am-I?" question turns out to be contained in part in the answer to the question, "Who are we?" This leader's guide provides an opportunity for a group of Christians to grow together through a series of holistically Christ-centered experiences. Reading about and discussing Christian fellowship, for example, is as different from actually living it as reading about a steak is different from eating it.

Christian community is the body of Christ being itself. This leader's guide gives the careful guidance necessary to insure an enlightening and vitalizing experience of Christian growth.

Growth as Christians

Christianity is always a matter of growth. Learning the answer to the question, " Who am I as a Christian?" is not the end; it is the beginning of a process. Christianity is constant movement from the old selfishness toward the new person in Christ.

Too often, we think that once a certain body of knowledge has been learned, we have "arrived." Not so! Growth in your Christian life continues until the day you die. It is true that you cannot make yourself grow in the Christian faith. Nevertheless, you can put yourself in places where "God can give the growth." The course in this guide is one such place.

Making Theology Practical

Both authors have always had a penchant for the practical. This is not to minimize the intellectual. It's just that "theology" that cannot be put into practice is no theology at all. God did not talk about creating. God created! The Christian does not merely talk about caring. The Christian cares! *Christian Caregiving—a Way of Life* is a call to action. This leader's guide answers that call by providing experiences and an environment that enable us to care on a practical level.

Training Specific Groups in the Congregation

Since all of the Church is called to care for the world, almost every group in a church can benefit from this training resource. Evangelism teams, boards of elders or deacons, teachers, new member classes, inactive member teams, church governing bodies, and many other groups could thus become more effective.

Evangelism

Evangelism is an embrace, not a club. As you are embraced by the love of God, you cannot help but embrace others. Indeed, these are the two pieces of the evangelism puzzle: applying the good news to yourself and sharing the good news with others.

God loves us even when we hate God. God entered our world and died. For us! For you! For the whole world! And when Jesus rose, he showed us that even death was incapable of separating us from his love. Now that's good news! In fact, that is just what the word *evangelizing* means—"good news-ing" someone.

But how can sharing this good news become a natural part of our lives? Those who take this course will so experience God's love and care that the dynamite of the gospel will demolish the obstacles that prevent us from sharing God's love with others. We will come to share naturally what so delights us. The unique content of *Christian Caregiving—a Way of Life* facilitates this.

Multiplication

This leader's guide enables multiplication of effort. From the first study group can come leaders for new groups. The pattern repeats as new leaders emerge from subsequent groups. There is a built-in expansion potential that makes these groups self-perpetuating.

We hope that the foregoing rationale for developing this leader's guide gives you a flavor of the transforming power that can enter into the people who grasp this experience and incorporate it into their "becomingness" as Christians. As you lead your group through *Christian Caregiving—a Way of Life*, may you find a sense of joy and fulfillment in experiencing the body of Christ.

KENNETH C. HAUGK
WILLIAM J. McKAY

INTRODUCTION

The approach of this guide is holistic. Holistic education is no simple matter. It involves the integration of intellectual, emotional, relational, and spiritual elements. You will be encouraging your participants to think, to react, to participate, to relate to each other and to the material under consideration in a variety of ways. Education is too often envisioned as merely a cognitive intellectual exercise. Leading an educational experience that is more than mere cognition might be unfamiliar ground for you. Therefore, this introduction and the 20 chapter-modules are very explicit. We want you to do the best possible job of teaching your people holistically.

Who Will Use This Manual?

The pastor or another member of the church staff might well be one of the instructors the first time this course is offered. The presence of this person can lend authority, credibility, and stability to the group. Other appropriate group leaders include those already involved in adult education in your congregation who have taught similar classes. Whomever you choose to lead this experience, select the teacher(s) with care.

Remember that from an initial group those with leadership qualities might emerge who are capable of leading subsequent groups. The class becomes self-perpetuating.

You might also consider team-teaching the course. The structure and method of this leader's guide accommodate themselves very well to team-teaching. This should not be an excuse, however, for any leader to be absent from a session. The presence of all instructors at every session is imperative because of the group dynamics of the class, not to mention that their absence sets a bad example.

It is also vital to the success of your group that the leaders be just that: leaders. Although the leaders are certainly a part of the group, they are simultaneously apart from it. As with any class, and perhaps somewhat more with this one, each session needs to keep moving. The group needs to be kept "on the track" while still having opportunities for creative expressions. One specific leadership function is guiding the group so that no one person dominates the class time.

Structuring Your Sequence of Sessions

Christian Caregiving—a Way of Life contains 20 chapters. This leader's guide provides 20 self-contained sets of resources for processing each chapter (each called a "chapter-module" from now on). Each chapter-module will take about one hour to work through, totaling 20 hours for the entire sequence.

We recommend that you schedule the course across ten weeks (or seven weeks if a weekend retreat is included—see pages 18, 19) and cover two chapter-modules in a 2½-hour session each week. The extra half hour will give you time for an opening devotion and a 15- to 20-minute break. This is a structure that thousands of previous classes have found to be satisfactory.

The 10-week course can be a special education and growth offering. Members of your congregation will need to sign up for it. Commitment is important. Advise all would-be participants that the nature of the experience necessitates attendance at all sessions.

Will individuals commit themselves to 10 sessions? Yes! Experience indicates that people are yearning for a number of elements included in this education, growth, and training sequence. They want a chance to discover the uniqueness of the Christian lifestyle.

One key to commitment and good attendance is to clarify expectations ahead of time. People appreciate and respect this. You might think that you will not have enough people sign up if these expectations are announced. Not so. Rather than having a problem with too few people signing up, you could find yourself with the happy dilemma of having to turn people away with the suggestion that they wait for the next time you offer the experience.

Another possibility is to schedule your session during the one-hour Sunday morning adult education time. This means a total of 20 weeks to cover the entire sequence of chapter-modules, which might or might not be practical, depending on attendance patterns. You can determine best whether this plan will work.

Getting Your Group Together

Scheduling—Time of Day. A natural time to meet would be the evening. You might want to meet from 7:00 to 9:30 P.M., 7:30 to 10:00 P.M., or whatever is normal for your church and area. Another possibility would be to run a daytime group, perhaps during the morning hours of 9:30 A.M. to 12:00 noon.

When you pick a time, stick to it. Start promptly and end promptly. Participants' enthusiasm for the class can lull you into thinking it is okay to let a meeting drag on for 10 or 20 minutes longer. Don't do it! There is at least one person concerned about a baby-sitter who needs to get home. There is another who needs to get up early the next day, and so on. It is also much better to have people hungry for more.

Scheduling—Time of Year. Here are some possible beginning and ending dates. Adjust them according to your own situation.

September 15–November 15: This is when church programs traditionally get off the ground as people get back into the swing of things after the summer.

November 1–December 15 and January 1–February 1: With a possible one-week break at Thanksgiving and a two-week break at Christmas, this is another viable option. You might schedule a holiday celebration for the group during one of the Christmas weeks when you are not meeting for class.

January 10–March 10: This might be a good time, when the flurry of holiday activities is past. In the midst of northern winters, the class could provide an oasis of warmth.

April 15–June 15: Beginning after Easter and ending before your congregation scatters for the summer, this could be a meaningful way to wrap up the church year.

If 10 weekly sessions don't quite fit into the time available, inclusion of a retreat can reduce the number of weeks to seven (see pp. 18, 19).

Publicity and Recruitment. Publicity and recruitment are closely related. The more thorough your publicity efforts, the more effectively you will be able to recruit for the course. Complete helps for publicity are located in Appendix A beginning on page 159.

In publicizing the course for the first time, you might choose to use "Sample Letter 1: The First Time the Class Is Offered." This letter could be used as part of a monthly newsletter or as a special mailing. Announce subsequent offerings of the class with a letter such as "Sample Letter 2: For Subsequent Offerings of the Course." Additionally, you can make use of bulletin inserts or announcements, posters, and verbal announcements. Inform special groups in the congregation also of the unique benefits the course offers them. Signs on the church grounds, news releases to local papers, and public service announcements to local radio stations can serve to publicize the course to the community.

Group Size. Such variables as leader's preference, meeting room size, demand, and congregational precedent all figure into determining the ideal size for your class. These are things you must consider, weighing the advantages and disadvantages. This leader's guide is structured to work well in a class of *any* size. Our own preference, however, is to work with a group large enough to insure a variety of participants for small group work, yet small enough that, by the final session, everyone knows everyone else by name—in other words, a group of 15-40 people.

Age of Participants. The crucial factor in determining the age of participants is individual maturity rather than chronological age. Many young adults from their junior year in high school are quite mature and make welcome additions to the group.

If a number of young people are interested in this experience, conduct a specific class geared toward their needs and concerns. Slight (but obvious) modifications of this guide would be required.

Conducting the Sessions

Confidentiality. Remind all participants from the beginning that strict confidentiality is necessary. What has been shared by an individual must not be repeated unless that person gives express permission for its repetition. Even then, discretion is imperative. Knowing from the start that everyone has agreed to confidentiality can promote the trust needed for group members to share sensitive matters that will promote growth and understanding.

In addition, emphasize that participants should talk about *their own* feelings and experiences, not those of others.

Attendance. As mentioned previously, establish a policy of required attendance for the following reasons:

- The nature of this course and the group dynamics involved necessitate that all be present for every session. If individuals miss one or more sessions, they will miss out on certain holistic growth experiences. Furthermore, their reentry might be viewed as an intrusion by other members of the group.
- If you demonstrate the absolute seriousness with which you regard attendance, participants will respond in kind. People in the church are looking for experiences that can be taken seriously. The more committed you are to an attendance policy, the more enthusiastic people will be about the overall experience and the more they will get out of it.
- It is important that your people understand that this material is vital for those who wish to function as more congruent Christians. For full exposure to the material, mandatory attendance is a necessity.

Practically, we suggest that there be a sign-up process in which people register for the sequence, and by their registration indicate commitment to attend all sessions. This means there should be no visitors "dropping in" on one or two sessions. This could be very destructive to the trust level of those in the group who are already beginning to develop bonds among themselves.

Of course you will need to set an example with your own consistent attendance. Anything less will destroy the commitment your group professes. There might be a temptation to "slip out" occasionally, especially when another person team-teaches with you. Don't do it! It will come back to haunt you and the whole group. You should be absent only for the most severe emergencies, those that absolutely cannot be delayed.

Except for illness or the necessity to be out of town, expect attendance to be close to 100 percent. An *esprit de corps*, a bond of Christian community, will develop that makes people want to attend.

Materials. The participants need a copy of *Christian Caregiving—a Way of Life*, a notepad, and a pen or pencil. Each leader will need the same plus this leader's guide. The meeting room should be equipped with a chalkboard, flip chart, or overhead projector. For some exercises you will need other easily acquired items. These will be indicated in the session directions.

Assignments. It would certainly be beneficial for all participants to have read the assignment ahead of time; however, that is not an absolute necessity. Because of the way each chapter-module is designed, even a participant who has not read a certain chapter ahead of time will still be able to gain much from that session.

Your participants should have very little trouble completing the reading assignment each week. Each 2½-hour session requires them to read two chapters, which average about seven to nine pages—less than 20 pages per week. Even when you have a retreat in which six chapter-modules are covered, there shouldn't be a great deal of difficulty completing the 50- or 60-page assignment.

Retreats. One of the most meaningful and enjoyable experiences for your class can be a retreat. A retreat is time away from ordinary life patterns to study, reflect, and "become," both as individuals and as a group.

You can speed up the bonding process and deepen the overall group experience by having a retreat. One enthusiastic instructor of a group that field-tested this leader's guide before publication commented:

> Our retreat this past weekend was great! I know you greatly encourage retreats. Too bad retreats can't be made mandatory. I think our group really jelled as a result and it was a great experience for all.

Including one or more retreats can also shorten the number of weeks needed to complete this course. For example, if you are conducting your sequence with ten 2½-hour sessions, a retreat might reduce the number of weeks that you meet to seven. Remember to remind your group to read ahead. The number of chapters considered on a retreat will be about three times the length of the average assignment.

How can retreats be structured? One very workable time schedule is to bring the group together Friday night and all day Saturday. You might want to begin with a common meal (a potluck supper, for example) on Friday followed by a 2- or 2½-hour evening session. Your group can meet again on Saturday morning for another 2½-hour session followed by a similar session in the afternoon. A total of six chapter-modules can be covered with this schedule.

Where would be a good place to meet? It is always appropriate to meet at a retreat or conference center. This might not be feasible, however, depending on such variables as cost and distance. While retreat centers have many benefits, little of the sense of community is lost if the retreat is held at the church. The decisive factor is *just getting together for that extended block of time.* Where you meet and whether the group stays overnight is secondary: just having the retreat is the essential.

Resources for Processing Each Chapter

Five basic steps are contained within each chapter-module:

1. Opening Prayer (or opening devotion)—1-5 minutes
2. Lead-In—1-2 minutes
3. Discussion Questions—10-20 minutes
4. Experiential Learning Exercises—30-45 minutes
5. Closing—1-2 minutes

In each chapter-module, a number of goals are provided, focusing on growth targets for that module. The goals draw from the essence of the particular chapter, coupled with working through the material in class. They are holistic in scope, having cognitive, emotional, social, behavioral, and spiritual emphases. Part of your task as leader is to choose a good mix of "Discussion Questions" and "Experiential Learning Exercises" so that the widest possible variety of goals is covered.

We suggest that you keep the goals to yourself, at least at the beginning of each module. Mentioning the goals ahead of time could spoil the excitement for the group members as they go through the exercises.

Five Resources

1. Opening Prayer. Each chapter-module contains a brief prayer relating to the content of the chapter under consideration. Feel free to adapt or substitute a prayer of your own.

Having a devotion is another option. It could be led by a leader or group member. You might want to do the first one (or more) yourself and, after that, encourage group members to become involved.

If you are covering two chapters in a single class session (the recommended structure of this leader's guide), you will end up with two "Opening Prayers" for each session. You might want to combine the two prayers into one for use at the beginning of the session. Another possibility would be to open the first and second halves of the 2½-hour session with the appropriate prayer.

2. Lead-In. Each of the 20 chapter-modules contains an introductory paragraph or two. Following the "Opening Prayer" or devotion, you can read the "Lead-In" verbatim to your group, or paraphrase. The Lead-In provides initial grounding, direction, and momentum as you process a chapter.

3. Discussion Questions. Each chapter-module contains questions designed to initiate discussion of major themes covered in the corresponding chapter of the book. More discussion questions are provided than you will have time to use. Restrict this segment to approximately one-third of the time spent on the entire chapter-module—no more than 20 minutes.

Pay attention to how you ask the questions. The way you speak the questions can do a lot to enhance or detract from a successful discussion. Be assertive in asking the questions. Show your interest and enthusiasm for the question by your tone of voice. Demonstrate your warmth and care for the members of your group by the way you speak. Read the questions as if you were asking them of your closest friends.

If the discussion lags . . . there are several things you might try:

- Keep quiet in the face of silence. The worst fault of most leaders and teachers is that they talk too much. Participants need thinking time before they respond to most questions. Allow class members to struggle a bit. Don't continually jump in and rescue the group with your version of the right answer.
- Subdivide a multiple-part question if you sense that the class is not understanding it. Help the group focus on just one part of the question at a time.

- If a question evokes little or no response, you may choose to just leave it and move on.
- It is, at times, appropriate to answer a question yourself. In doing this you can model the depth of thought, openness, and personal vulnerability you hope to see in the group members as they answer questions.
- If discussion seems to be winding down on one question, move on to the next one. It is better to leave a question slightly under-discussed than to overdiscuss it.

Be aware of time. It is important to keep your class moving and not bog down in any particular segment.

- Discussion is meant to occupy, *at most*, one-third of the class time. If you give in to the temptation to use a lot more time for discussion questions, your group will miss out on other learning that is just as valuable. At times it can be tempting to stick with the intellectual learning by stretching out the discussion time instead of moving on to the Experiential Learning Exercises. Don't succumb to this temptation. Both kinds of learning are needed and valuable.
- If you are running out of discussion time, don't try to rush through "one last question." It is better to thoroughly discuss two questions than it is to rush through three or four. If you just have a few minutes left, end the discussion time and move on to the Experiential Learning Exercises early.
- Leaders of groups that field-tested this material indicated that they were able to discuss an average of three to four questions for each chapter-module in the allotted time.

Don't get caught in endless arguments. It is not helpful to go on and on arguing about a point that will never be resolved anyway. If you or others in your group get stuck in an argument, say something like, "We can agree to disagree," or, "It is okay that we have differing ideas about this," and move the group to another question or activity. You can terminate a discussion that's going nowhere by saying, "I'm getting anxious about giving everyone a chance to participate, so I think we'll move on now."

4. Experiential Learning Exercises. Learning while experiencing is an exciting and productive part of the whole education and growth process. Experiential exercises also effectively cause learning and growth to take place in "deep" ways. Educators know that the more senses of the entire person involved in the learning process, the deeper and more permanent the learning is.

More "Experiential Learning Exercises" are provided for each chapter-module than could possibly (or desirably) be used in the suggested 60-minute time period. Pick and choose from the resources provided to meet the needs of your own group.

Do not rush through an exercise in order to get on to others. It is much better to do a few exercises thoroughly. A "squeeze-them-in" approach leads only to frustration on the part of the participants, who would then not receive any real, in-depth, experiential learning. On the other hand, do not let the exercises drag on.

At times, experiential exercises can seem threatening to some individuals, especially at the beginning. The majority of the exercises in this leader's guide are conservative in their design. They balance maximum growth and participation of individuals with a minimum of threatening elements. Furthermore, the earlier chapter-modules are constructed more conservatively, allowing the participants some time to become acquainted. You might find that some participants are reluctant to become involved in these exercises. Use them without apology. Often these initially reticent people are among the first to report back to group leaders how much they have enjoyed the exercises despite initial anxiety. If you sense that someone is very uncomfortable with an exercise, tell the group that if anyone wants to say "pass," he or she may. Always respect the individual's freedom.

Since you will inevitably be faced with the situation of having groups that are not cleanly divisible into twos, threes, fives, etc., common sense will dictate what to do with the leftover people. Some exercises can easily have larger, some smaller groups. The main thing is to make sure that no one is excluded.

Taking a group through experiential exercises can be a very sensitive matter. It is for this reason that the exercises are all very complete, including what is to be spoken to the group. Therefore, feel free to simply read the instructions verbatim.

A. *Small Group Exercises.* A good size for a small group is five. Five is large enough to provide a variety of views, and yet small enough to permit everyone to participate. Each time you break your large group into smaller groups, encourage the participants to form a group with people they do not know well.

It is essential whenever you break your large group into small groups that you ask each group to choose a convener or leader before proceeding with the exercise. That person will be responsible for keeping the group on track and focusing on the agenda on hand. For example, if several brainstorming questions on a topic are assigned, that person will be responsible for making sure that the group does not bog down on one question. Conveners can be the crucial element making or breaking your small group work. They are, in effect, the ones in the small group where "the buck stops passing." They can and should participate as much as the others, but they are the ones who insure that things function smoothly and stay focused.

B. *Dyad/Triad Exercises.* A number of chapter-modules include dyad (pairs) or triad (three persons) exercises. When the group is broken up into pairs, the major positive feature is that each person is actively involved at all times in the interaction. An advantage of triads is that while two people might be involved, for example, practicing a caring and relating skill, the third person can act as a commentator. It is important when a triad is formed that all members of the triad have the opportunity to switch roles.

C. *Self-Discovery Exercises.* Some chapter-modules contain exercises that provide opportunity for the participants to do some self-exploration in addition to relating. These are mostly "pencil and pad" exercises in which participants respond to questions and reflect on these answers. These start out as individual writing exercises and often move into opportunities for small group relating.

D. *Imaging Exercises.* Several chapter-modules contain opportunities for class members to close their eyes and get in touch with the topic and themselves through their imagination. These are often good to use at the beginning or the end of the exercises.

5. Closing. For each chapter-module, a "Closing" has been provided that draws from the content of each chapter. It is a blessing or benediction to be spoken or read by you at the conclusion of your work on that chapter. As with the "Opening Prayers," you will have two separate "Closings" when you cover two chapter-modules in one session. You might want to use one "Closing" right before the break and another at the end of the session, use only one of them at the end of the session, or combine the two "Closings" into one.

CHAPTER-MODULE 1

It's Not Easy

Goals

Participants may:

1-A Experience God's forgiveness for their failings so they can risk offering to others distinctively Christian care.

1-B Gain confidence in expressing their Christian distinctiveness to others.

1-C Learn that others also have difficulty expressing their Christian distinctiveness.

1-D Help others in the class experience more fully their relationship with God.

1-E "Break the ice" in experiencing Christian community.

1-F Learn how body language can create an atmosphere of acceptance or rejection.

Opening Prayer

Note to Leader: Remember that you might have longer opening devotions, with class members leading them as time goes on.

Lord God, you have declared that it is in our weakness that you are strong. Help us as we struggle with the difficulties we face in offering others distinctively Christian caring and relating. Help us avoid embarrassment, unrealistic fear of rejection, excessive caution, and uncertainty as you replace our weakness with your great strength. Help us to live for you, serve you by serving others, and let you live through us in our distinctively Christian caregiving, in Jesus' name. Amen.

Lead-In

Note to Leader: The lead-in for this first chapter-module is significantly longer than the other lead-ins because this one serves to introduce the entire course, providing rationale and general direction. For this reason, you may need to adjust slightly the time devoted to other parts of this chapter-module.

Welcome in the name of Jesus! In the weeks ahead, we will gather together to study and learn, so that we may offer a higher quality of distinctively Christian caregiving than ever before. Our goal is to understand Christian caring better, so that we may care more effectively, more efficiently, more as Christ himself cares. We are gathering here not just to become more effective learners in Christ's school, but also to become more effective servants in God's realm.

To this end I am going to spend a few minutes outlining some of the rationale for our time together. What is this course all about? What are the benefits for us? And how can we translate what we learn here into better Christian caring and relating to others? Here are six points that will answer these and other pertinent questions about our intensive look at *Christian Caregiving—a Way of Life*.

The Crucial Nature of the Content. Books typically fall in and out of a person's life as isolated events unless there is some immediate call to action. How many times have you read a book and shelved it saying, "There's some great stuff in here, and some day I'm going to do that." But do you? The material in *Christian Caregiving—a Way of Life* speaks for itself, and I suspect that most readers will feel compelled to go beyond the reading stage and be itching to "do something."

In our time together, we are going to scratch that itch. We want to underscore the message of *Christian Caregiving—a Way of Life* and extend it into our lives and experiences. The purpose of *Christian Caregiving—a Way of Life* is to equip us for distinctively Christian life-styles of caring and relating. One major obstacle as Christians in reaching this end seems to be an "identity crisis." We may be eager to be "distinctively Christian," but not know exactly what this means. Distinctively Christian caring and relating is neither *optional* nor *desirable* for followers of Jesus. It is *necessary!* Imagine a fish trying to live outside its native environment. That's unthinkable. The "native environment" of Christians is the world of caring and relating, and it is imperative for Christians to recognize this reality and act consistently with it. Yet, we often fail to be distinctively Christian in our caring and relating. This book directly confronts that dilemma, striving not only to acquaint us with our "natural environment of Christian caring," but also instilling a love for it. This book and our study will move us to a deeper understanding of our lives and identities as Christians, a deeper understanding that will inevitably bear fruit in more loving service in the world.

"Who Am I, Anyway?" One of the important questions Christians continue to ask is, "Who am I as a Christian, anyway?" This question is often asked with overtones of puzzled bewilderment and occasional self-dislike. Answers abound, but you still might find yourself thinking, "Yes, but who am I . . . really?"

From the secular world, we are confronted with every imaginable kind of influence, philosophy, methodology, and approach to life. These are by no means all bad; many are quite good. Yet the distinctively Christian consciousness can all too easily be lost in the shuffle. Together we are about to make a concerted effort to remedy that situation by raising Christian consciousness and promoting Christian practice.

None of us wants merely to be told who we are; we want to experience it. I hope our words and actions here will help us internalize our Christian self-identity.

An Experience in Christian Community. Second only to the question "Who am I?" is the question "Who are we?" We are about to have a holistically Christ-centered group experience. Rather than just thinking and talking about Christian fellowship, we will experience it together. Discussing Christian fellowship is as different from actually living it as talking about an apple is different from eating it. Christian community is the body of Christ in action, and experiencing it can be vital and energizing for all of us.

Growing as Christians. Our Christianity is always a matter of growth. Learning the answer to the question "Who am I as a Christian?" is not the end; it is the beginning of a process. Christianity is constant movement from the not-yet to the now. It is moving away from the old selfishness to the new people whom Christ has created.

Too often, we imagine that mastering a certain body of knowledge means that we've "arrived." Not so! Growth in our Christian lives cannot cease with the end of formal religious instruction. It continues until the day we die. Although we cannot force ourselves to grow in the Christian faith, we can put ourselves in places where "God can give the growth." Right here is one of those places.

Making Theology Practical. The author of *Christian Caregiving—a Way of Life* has always had a penchant for the practical, which resulted in his developing the Stephen Series system of lay caring ministry. Rather than minimizing the intellectual, he asserts that "theology" that cannot be put into practice is no theology at all. Theology is *always* practical. God didn't just talk about creating. He created! Likewise, Christians don't merely talk about caring. We care! The book, *Christian Caregiving—a Way of Life* is our call to action. This time together will enable us to answer that call in concrete ways.

Evangelism. Evangelism is an embrace, not a club. As we are embraced by the love of God, we cannot help but embrace others. Indeed, these are the two pieces of the evangelism puzzle: applying the good news to ourselves, and sharing the good news with others.

God loves us even when we hate him. He entered our world and died. For me! For you! For the whole world! And when he rose, he showed us that death itself was incapable of separating us from his love. Now that's good news! In fact, that's precisely what the word *evangelizing* means—"good news-ing" someone.

But how do we share this good news? Why aren't we doing more of it? Why doesn't this sharing seem natural, appropriate, and comfortable to us? Here's where our group experience comes in. We will experience a little bit of God's love and care here in this group, and that warming gospel might just melt some of the obstacles that prevent us from sharing God's love with others.

In our first session, we look at the difficulties we experience in caring and relating in distinctively Christian ways. We are going to try to understand some of these difficulties so that, with God's help, we can overcome them. You will discover that you are not alone in experiencing them. We will draw strength from each other and from

God as we learn now and in future sessions to live and relate in distinctively Christian ways.

Discussion Questions

Note to Leader: Devote one-third of the time *at most* to "Discussion Questions." The numbers and letters in parentheses indicate which goals the "Discussion Questions" or "Experiential Learning Exercises" refer to.

A. What might Peter L. have said about his Christian beliefs in response to his friends' mockery of the "sidewalk preacher"? *(1-B, 1-C)*
B. Have you had experiences in which you were able to share your faith with someone and felt good about it? Relate one of these experiences. *(1-B, 1-D)*
C. Can you recall experiences in which you wanted to share your faith verbally with someone, but didn't? If so, what kept you from sharing? *(Discuss. Then ask:)* What would have made it easier to share? *(1-C, 1-D)*
D. "The Lord isn't merely gritting his teeth and using imperfect humans: he likes it that way!" *(Christian Caregiving—a Way of Life,* p. 12) What does this mean for you in your caring and relating? *(1-A, 1-B)*
E. What is "explosive," as the author states on p. 15, about Christian resources? *(1-D)*
F. How can sensitive listening on your part reduce the chance of someone rejecting your distinctively Christian behavior toward them? *(1-B)*
G. How does God's forgiveness relate to our risk taking as Christian caring persons? *(1-A, 1-D)*

Experiential Learning Exercises

Note to Leader: Devote half or more of the time in this and other chapter-modules to the "Experiential Learning Exercises." We strongly recommend using the first two exercises.

1. A Picture of Caring (1-B, 1-E)

Time: 10-15 minutes
Grouping: Alone at first, then groups of three
Materials: Paper and crayons, felt-tip pens, or pencils

Leader: *Distribute materials. Ask each person to find a space to work alone. Say:*
   "Each of you spend five minutes alone creating a picture of what Christian caring looks like. Use stick figures if you wish. Somehow show how you perceive Christian caring. Remember that this is not an art contest. Your ideas are what is important, not your artistic ability. Go ahead."
   (Call time after five minutes. Ask the class to form groups of three. Say:)
   "Each group choose a convener. That person has the job of making sure you stay on track." *(Wait until the groups have chosen conveners. Then say:)* "Take two or three minutes each to share your drawing and explain its meaning. I'll call time at three-minute intervals, so you will know it's about time for the next person to begin. Go ahead."
   (Wrap up the sharing in threesomes after 10 minutes. It's better to have some groups eager to continue than to have others waiting for them to finish. Use your own judgment about whether to allow an extra minute or so.)

Note to Leader: You might want to have participants remain in their same groups for the next exercise, if you choose to do it.

2. Popping the Question (1-B, 1-E)

Time: 10-12 minutes
Grouping: Groups of three

Leader: *Ask the class to form groups of three. Say:*
   "Each group choose a convener, who should have a watch. That person has the job of making sure you stay on track and stick to the time limits and especially keeping the discussion focused on the subject at hand."

(Selecting a convener is very important because in small groups like this it is very easy to get sidetracked. The convener's job is to make sure the group does not get sidetracked. Pause until a convener is selected.)

Note to Leader: The purpose of this situation is to put group members in a setting where they must pick the one or two most important aspects to them, not anyone else!—of their faith. It is to bring people very quickly to addressing the question: What is the core of your faith?

"I'm going to set up a situation for you. You're at the airport. You have taken a good friend there, one who has never asked you about your faith before, never even talked about religion. The person has *only one minute* before getting on the plane. Suddenly he or she says, 'What's your Christianity all about?' and you have just one minute to respond. What do you say? Each of you in turn take one minute to actually say to the others what you would say. Conveners, cut each speaker off with a last-call boarding announcement when one minute is up. Go ahead."

(At the end of about five minutes, open up discussion to the larger group for about five minutes.)

3. Shy Faith (1-A, 1-C)

Time: 10-15 minutes
Grouping: Pairs
Advance Preparation: Write the following ahead of time on an overhead or chalkboard, in a place where you can hide it until it's time to show it to the class.

Share a time when you were embarrassed about your faith. Do you wish you had responded differently in this situation? If so, how?

Leader: *Ask the class to gather into pairs. When the pairs are situated around the room, facing each other, say:*

"One of you share your answer to these questions for three or four minutes while the other listens. Then you'll switch roles and the first will listen while the second shares. I'll call time when half the time is up so you know when the other should begin. Go ahead."

(Let them know when half the time has elapsed so they can switch roles. At the end of three or four minutes, say:)

"Switch roles now and let the other person respond to these questions."

(*When everyone has had a turn, discuss the exercise for a few minutes with the group as a whole. The participants can remain in their pairs for the discussion. The leader could use one or both of the following questions to focus the discussion:*)

1. How can we overcome the factors that keep us from being distinctively Christian in our caring and relating?
2. How can we be certain that we do not become obnoxious or insensitive in our distinctively Christian relating?

4. Five Difficulties (1-C)

Time: 20-25 minutes
Grouping: Alone at first, then groups of five
Materials: Paper, pen or pencil, their copies of *Christian Caregiving—a Way of Life*. If possible, have a flip chart and markers for each group of five.

Leader: *Read the following:*

"Take about five minutes to write down five difficulties you have experienced in trying to live and care in a distinctively Christian manner. You will have the opportunity to share these with the other members of your group. If you need ideas, turn to pages 13-18 in *Christian Caregiving—a Way of Life* and look over the author's discussion of 11 difficulties. Go ahead."

(*Inform the class when one minute remains. At the end of five minutes, ask the class to assemble into groups of five. Wait for this to happen. Then say:*)

"Now each group choose someone as a recorder."

(*Pause until this has happened. Then say:*)

"Take turns sharing what you have written down. Whoever is recording should write down a one- or two-word summary of each difficulty mentioned. After everyone has contributed, compare the difficulties that each of you have shared. See if you can discover similarities among each other's difficulties. Take 10 more minutes. You can begin."

(*If you like, conclude the exercise by discussing it briefly with the whole class.*)

5. Listen to Me (1-F)

Time: 10-12 minutes
Grouping: Pairs

Leader: *Ask the class to assemble into pairs. After that have the partners designate one person as* A *and the other as* B. *Then say:*

"I would like person *A* to tell *B* something very important about his or her faith. Person *B*, please act uncomfortable especially through your body language. As you listen, do as many of these behaviors as possible:

- Avoid eye contact.
- Turn your chair to the side, away from person *A*.
- Doodle.
- Look at your watch.
- Examine your fingernails with great interest.
- Fold your arms and lean away from person *A*.
- Yawn.
- Interrupt person *A*; finish his or her sentences.
- Make irrelevant comments or change the topic.

Do this for one minute. Go ahead."
  (After one minute say:)
  "Each of you now share how you felt about what you just did."
  (After two or three minutes say:)
  "Now would *B* please share with *A* something very important about your faith. Person *A*, pay very close attention and be very interested.

- Show by your posture and eye contact that you are hanging on person *B*'s every word.
- Say um-hmm and other sounds that show you understand what person *B* is saying.
- Do what you can to encourage the other person to say more.

Do this for one minute. You can begin now."
  (After one minute say:)
  "Again share how you felt about what you did. Go ahead."
  (After two to three minutes, bring the exercise to a close or discuss briefly with the class as a whole.)

6. Difficulties (1-B, 1-C)

Time: 10-15 minutes
Grouping: Groups of three
Materials: Their copies of Christian Caregiving—a Way of Life

Leader: *Ask the class to assemble into groups of three and arrange their chairs to face one another. Say:*
"Now choose a convener to lead the discussion."
(Pause for a moment for this to happen. Then read the following:)
"Turn to Chapter 1 in *Christian Caregiving—a Way of Life* and look over the author's discussion of the 11 difficulties on pages 13-18. Go ahead, take a couple of minutes to glance through them."
(Pause two minutes, then continue.)
"Now, share with each other some of the difficulties you have experienced in your attempt to be distinctively Christian. The ones you come up with might or might not be listed in the chapter. It doesn't matter who starts, but all of you should take the opportunity to share some of the problems you have experienced in being distinctively Christian. We'll take about 10 minutes. Go ahead and begin."
(Inform the class at three-minute intervals.)

7. Walking with Christ in Distinctively Christian Caregiving (1-B, 1-D)

Time: 15 minutes
Grouping: Pairs
Materials: Bibles for each pair
Advance Preparation: Make enough slips, each with one of the Bible passages on it, to have one for each pair in your class. You will also either need to write the questions on the chalkboard or, better, make a copy of them to give to each pair.

Leader: *Ask the class to assemble in pairs, with at least one Bible per pair. Give each pair one of the following Scripture passages and ask them to read it and then to answer the four questions you provide.*

Scriptures:	The Last and the First	Matthew 20:1-16
	Whom to Pay What?	Matthew 22:15-22
	The Talents	Matthew 25:14-30
	Who Is the Greatest?	Mark 9:33-37

The Good Samaritan	Luke 10:25-37
The Prodigal Son	Luke 15:11-32
The Adulterous Woman	John 7:53, 8:1-11

Questions:

1. In your Scripture passage identify the caregivers and the care receivers.
2. What qualities, attitudes, and values typify the successful caregiver in these Scriptures? What specific actions does Christ suggest for the successful caregiver in each Scripture?
3. What is distinctively Christian about the attitudes and actions Christ suggests in each of these Scripture passages?
4. How does Christ's suggested action coincide with or go against your normal ways of thinking and doing things?

Note to Leader: Sometime during your first meeting remind participants of the necessity to keep confidential anything they learn about other group members. You might want to say something like: "Confidentiality is a vital part of our experience together. To insure trust, honest communication, and freedom of expression for one another, it is essential that each of us commit to keep confidential everything shared by other participants. Our trustworthiness in this regard will benefit everyone's experience here."

Closing

May our God of strength be present in our weakness. May our God of forgiveness be present in our failings. May our God of encouragement be present as we try to serve him better. May God's peace and joy fill our hearts and inform our actions as we be and become the servants Christ both taught us and showed us how to be. Amen.

CHAPTER-MODULE 2

God as the Curegiver

Goals

Participants may:

2-*A* Perceive more accurately their responsibilities as caregivers.

2-*B* Move toward accepting God as the curegiver.

2-*C* See how it feels to turn the responsibility for curing over to God.

2-*D* Experience feelings of care *receivers* to gain better understanding of that perspective.

2-*E* See themselves as recipients of God's care and cure, and help others do the same.

2-*F* Experience Christian community.

Opening Prayer

Almighty God, you want us to share with others the love and care that you have given us. Without your help we are unable to do so. We rely totally on you to provide cure, healing, and growth in ourselves and in those we serve. Thank you for the blessing of your love for us and your willingness to travel the ultimate road— the road to the cross—that we, along with those we serve, might receive the ultimate cure. In Jesus' name. Amen.

Lead-In

Jesus said, "The harvest is plentiful, but the laborers are few; therefore ask the Lord of the harvest to send out laborers into his harvest" (Matt. 9:37-38). This is one of the many images that help us understand that we are partners with God in the work of caring for our world. We plant, tend, and harvest crops, but God causes the miracle of growth. We can care for others, but God produces the growth, the healing, the cure in people's lives. It is tempting at times to get so caught up in doing our part that we forget God's responsibility in the caring/curing process. But we must not forget God's centrality to the healing process. As Thomas à Kempis says, we must put God first. We must put ourselves, not second, but in God's hands: "O Lord, you know what is best for us, let this or that be done as you shall please. Give what you will, and how much, and when you will. Deal with me as you think good, and as best pleases you. Set me where you will, and deal with me in all things just as you will. Behold, I am your servant, prepared for all things; for I desire not to live unto myself, but unto you, and oh, that I could do it worthily and perfectly!" In this module, let us look at the division of responsibilities in the healing process, and grow in appreciation of God's way of using us in *God's* process of caring and curing.

Discussion Questions

A. Look at the discussion of the word *therapy* on page 20. In that sense, would you say Jesus was a therapist? How? *(Discuss. Then ask:)* What biblical evidence might there be for this conclusion? *(2-A, 2-B)*

B. Can you recall experiences in which you "planted and watered" and God gave the growth (i.e., a cure)? How did you plant and water? *(2-A, 2-B)*

C. Have you ever had an experience where you viewed yourself as a curegiver rather than a caregiver? What happened? *(2-A, 2-B)*

D. Have you ever had an experience when you completely trusted God to help you with a specific problem or event? What happened? *(2-E)*

E. How might you answer one who says it is irresponsible to say that only God is able to give results? (2-A, 2-B)

F. How would you answer someone who says, "Well, if God is the curegiver, I'll wait for God to send an angel to provide whatever my neighbor needs!" (2-A)

G. Think of one person at home, at work, in your neighborhood, who is in need of care. How might you be a Christian therapist to that person? (2-A)

Experiential Learning Exercises

1. I Thought It Was Up to Me (2-C)

Time: 15 minutes
Grouping: Pairs

Leader: *Divide the class into pairs. Have the pairs scatter around the room and arrange their chairs so that they are facing each other. Designate one person to be A, the other to be B. Read the following:*

"Those of you who are A share with your partner a time in which you felt totally responsible for another person's change or progress. Take three or four minutes to explain what happened and how you felt about it. I'll let you know when about three minutes have elapsed. Go ahead."

(Inform the class when 30 seconds remain and then go on.)

"Those of you who are B now do the same thing: Share with A a situation where *you* felt totally responsible for another person's change. Tell A how you felt about it. Go ahead."

(After three or four minutes inform the class that 30 seconds remain, then go on.)

"The two of you discuss this: What difference do you think it would have made in your actions and words if you had placed the responsibility for progress in God's hands? Go ahead."

(Inform the class when 30 seconds remain and close the exercise after about five minutes.)

2. A Harvest of Cures (2-D, 2-E, 2-F)

Time: 20 minutes
Grouping: Groups of three
Advance Preparation: Write the following for all to see:
1. Share a time in your life when you were cured of something.
2. Relate what led up to the cure, how others may have "planted and watered."
3. Talk about how the cure finally came about.

Leader: *Ask the class to gather in groups of three. Have each group select a convener. Then read the following:*

"Would each of you in turn please respond to these three statements as best you can. (*Indicate the instructions you wrote in advance.*) You have 15 minutes or so. I will inform you at five-minute intervals. Remember, you can pass if you wish. Go ahead."

(*At the end of five and then ten minutes, say:*)

"Now the next person should begin sharing."

(*Gather everyone's attention after fifteen minutes total, and say:*)

"Even Jesus does not force his cures upon us. There's a great passage in Revelation 3:20 that describes God's discretion when it comes to offering the most beautiful cure of all."

(*Ask someone to look that passage up, or read it yourself. It is printed here for your convenience:*)

Listen! I am standing at the door, knocking; if you hear my voice and open the door, I will come in to you and eat with you, and you with me.

(*Ask:*)

"Why does Jesus knock? Why not send in the heavenly special forces, knock the door down, and tell everybody 'Hands up'?" (*Discuss briefly.*)

3. Practice Makes Better (2-B, 2-C)

Time: 15-20 minutes
Grouping: Groups of three
Advance Preparation: Write the following, but keep concealed.
1. Which of the helping situations seemed more effective? More caring? Why?
2. Would you label one as curegiving and the other as caregiving?

Leader: *Ask the class to gather in groups of three. Have them designate themselves as A, B, and C in each group. Then read the following:*

"We are going to practice some helping situations. In each of the three situations, two people will interact and the third will act as an observer. After each role play, there will be time for you to discuss what happened. In the first situation, A and B interact while C observes. Here is the situation. A, a week or so ago you broke your leg. Since then you have been in the hospital. Today is your first day home, and you are visited by B. *B, your task in this situation is to make A feel better.* Let's take about five minutes. Go ahead."

(Give them about five minutes. Inform them when 30 seconds remain, and then go on.)

"In this next situation, B you are feeling very depressed because you have just lost your job. A, your task is to observe. C, yours is to talk with B about his or her feelings. Your goal is *not* necessarily to get B back on his or her feet or to make B feel any better, but just to listen to him or her, enabling B to get his or her feelings out in the open. Let's take five minutes for this. Go ahead."

(Give them about five minutes. Inform them when 30 seconds remain and then show the two questions you wrote.)

"Discuss these questions in your group, taking about five minutes. Go ahead."

4. Curing the World's Ills (2-A, 2-B, 2-C)

Time: 25-30 minutes
Grouping: Individual, then pairs
Materials: Recent newspapers, paper and pen
Advance Preparation: In advance, write these questions on the chalkboard or an overhead, and keep concealed:
   "Which of your two approaches is more likely to be effective? Why?"

Leader: *Divide the class into pairs and give each person a newspaper section that contains at least a few articles or editorials. Then say the following:*

"Please quickly look over your newspaper articles and each of you select one in which you can identify a problem that needs attention. Then write notes describing two approaches to the problem, one through caring and one through curing. After five minutes working independently to prepare your proposals, I will give you three minutes each to explain the problem and your two approaches to your partner. Go ahead and work independently on your problem and your approaches to it."

(*Give participants a 30-second warning to end their preparation time and then invite them to begin sharing their approaches. Allow about three minutes each. When both partners have shared their approaches, say:*)

"With your partner, please answer the following questions." (*Show the questions you have prepared in advance.*)

"Which of your two approaches is more likely to be effective? Why?"

(*At the end of three or four minutes, ask the whole group:*)

"Did anyone find a problem where it seemed to make perfect sense to take a curing approach?" (*They may have. In general, problems related to "things" are suitable for curing approaches, while problems related to persons almost always benefit by a caring approach. Discuss briefly.*)

Closing

May God, our curegiver, give us strength and compassion for each other and for ourselves, along with the faith and wisdom to trust him alone to bring about cures. May God's unchanging love for us give us continual healing and joy. Amen.

CHAPTER-MODULE 3

God, You, and Me

Goals

Participants may:

3-A Be aware of God's presence in caring relationships.

3-B Experience the concept of the "wounded healer."

3-C Show God's continuous love to others in this group.

3-D Grow in awareness of God's presence in every aspect of their lives.

3-E Experience God's presence through the experience of Christian community.

3-F Practice caring for one another.

Opening Prayer

Jesus, you gave us a wonderful promise when you told us that you are always with us. Help us to trust and believe your promise. Increase our awareness of your presence. Teach us how to translate our reliance on you into our care for others. Help us to share your love with them in both our caring actions and words, so that they can experience your presence also. We ask this, trusting your promise. Amen.

Lead-In

The task of caring for others can be overwhelming. It can be a huge responsibility and should not be entered into alone. We are, however, never alone. God is with us. One of the most inspirational books ever written on this subject is Rabbi Harold S. Kushner's *When Bad Things Happen to Good People*. No matter how bad it gets, no matter how hard it is to believe, God is always with you!

How is God present? How can we benefit from that presence? How can others benefit through us? This will be an exciting module as we explore these questions and experience God's dynamic presence among us and within us.

Discussion Questions

Note to Leader: **Remind participants of their commitment to confidentiality before you begin your discussions.**

A. Look at the three ways of God's being with us described in *Christian Caregiving—a Way of Life*, pages 25-27. Do you picture God being with you in any of these ways? In any other ways? (*3-A, 3-D*)

B. What difference has it made to you when you have consciously acknowledged God's presence with you? (*3-D*)

C. What difference might the awareness of God's presence make to a person for whom you are caring? (*3-D*)

D. How might you, as a carer, be a "wounded healer" for someone? (*3-B*)

E. What do you think the apostle Paul meant when he said to "pray without ceasing" (1 Thessalonians 5:17)? (*3-C, 3-D*)

F. Have you ever specifically verbalized God's reality, presence, or care to someone? What happened? (*3-A*)

Experiential Learning Exercises

Note to Leader: **This exercise is a good way to begin the experiential part of this particular chapter-module.**

1. Thanks God, I Needed That (3D, 3E)

Time: 5 minutes
Grouping: Whole Group

Leader: *Ask the class to make themselves as comfortable as they can, closing their eyes and relaxing. Dim the lights if possible. Read the following in a calm voice:*

"God wants to comfort us, to bring peace into our more or less chaotic lives. He wants to hold us in the palm of his hand. Let's see if we can experience that care. Take a moment to relax. Breathe deeply."

(Take a deep breath yourself, exhale slowly, then say:)

"Get comfortable. Let go of the areas of tension in your body."

(Pause 10 seconds.)

"Now think of something that happened during the last couple of days that caused you to feel pressure, something at work or at home or somewhere else. Envision yourself lifting that stress up to God and asking God to take control of it. God says, 'Yes,' and you no longer have to bear that burden."

(Pause 10 seconds.)

"Now, envision yourself in the middle of all the demands that fragment you. Instead of feeling fragmented, begin to feel yourself being lifted up to God, and God reaching out to you, and taking hold of you, gently holding you, protecting you. Hear God say, 'Receive my peace. Do not worry about all that you must do. Do not feel guilt or inadequacy. Instead, know that I love you; I care for you. Nothing else in the world matters.' "

(Pause 10 seconds.)

"Let the feeling of God's care and peace fill you now. Let it replace your anxiety. Know that this is how God wants you to feel. Get to know this feeling. Store it somewhere inside you where you will be able to find it again and again. Go back to this feeling when you begin feeling stressed."

(Pause 10 seconds.)

"Slowly open your eyes now, and see the people around you. Know that they are cared for by God just as you are."

(Give people a moment to re-orient themselves.)

2. Close to God (3-E, 3-F)

Time: 8-10 minutes
Grouping: Pairs

Leader: *Divide the class into pairs. Have each pair designate one person to be* A, *the other to be* B. *Wait for this to happen. Then say:*

"I'd like person *A* to share with person *B* a time when you were particularly conscious of the presence of God, a time when God was very close to you. We'll take three to four minutes for this."

(After about four minutes, or earlier if they seem to be finished, say:)

"Person *B*, share a time when you felt particularly close to God. Again, we'll take a few minutes for this."

(When three to four minutes are up, say:)

"Finish your time together with a one- or two-sentence prayer of thanks for your partner's experience of closeness to God. Be sure to use your partner's name in your prayer."

Note to Leader: You might want to discuss this exercise for a few minutes with the group as a whole.

3. A Story of Wounded Healers (3-B, 3-E)

Time: 20-30 minutes
Grouping: Groups of 5-8
Advance Preparation: Write for all to see:
   Elements of Your Story
   • **the healer's wound**
   • **the care receiver's pain or struggle**
   • **the caring process**
   • **the outcome**

Leader: *Ask the class to gather in groups of five to eight individuals in circles around the room. When this has happened, say:*

"Now choose a convener who will keep you focused on the task and make sure everyone gets a chance to contribute." *(Pause for this selection. Then say:)* "I'd like each group to work together and write a fictitious story. Designate one person from your group as the person to record and tell the story, or think of a way to tell the story as a group. This story is to be about a person who is a wounded healer in his or her caregiving. In your story talk about the healer's wound, about the care receiver's pain or struggle, about the caring process, and about the outcome. You have 15 minutes to write your story. Later each group will get a chance to tell its story."

(After about 15 minutes, bring the exercise to a close, realizing that some groups might need a little extra time to finish. Have each group tell its story.)

4. Who Has Seen the Wind? (3-D)

Time: 20 minutes
Grouping: Whole group, individual, then whole group

Leader: *Begin by saying:* "None of us has ever seen the wind, yet we know it is there. How do we know it? We are each blessed with five senses, or if we have lost one or more of those senses, the others compensate. Think with me for a minute, sense by sense, of ways in which we know the wind is there, and together we will construct a poem out loud. Give me images to fill in the lines of our poem":

I see the wind in . . . *(have participants vocalize lines and images out loud).*

I hear the wind in . . . *(have participants vocalize lines and images out loud).*

I smell the wind in . . . *(have participants vocalize lines and images out loud).*

I taste the wind in . . . *(have participants vocalize lines and images out loud).*

I touch the wind in . . . *(have participants vocalize lines and images out loud).*

(Then say:)

"Now each of you take five minutes and write your own brief poem, except substitute the word *God* for the words *the wind.* I see God in . . . .

(After the five minutes are up, invite volunteers to share their poems with the group. Discuss briefly—five minutes—with the group. Ask one or more of the following:)

"How close is God in these poems? How present is God in our world? How present is God in our lives?"

Note to Leader: If you use the following exercise, it is a good one with which to conclude the Experiential Learning portion.

5. Practicing God's Presence (3-E)

Time: 10 minutes
Grouping: Whole group

Leader: *Begin with:*
  "Let's take a few minutes to practice the presence of God. We probably all know intellectually that God is present with us here in this room. But let's see if we can really experience God's presence in other ways.
  "Get as comfortable as you can. Close your eyes and begin to breathe slowly . . . deeply . . . rhythmically. . . . Enter deeply inside yourself. Try to get in touch with the love, the compassion, the care of God. God is present inside us. Some of us will find God in a small compartment in our soul, a place reserved just for God. Others will experience God as a brightness and a warmth wherever we turn. Some of us may not feel God's presence at all, and we may feel sadness at what we have lost, or frustration at what we have never found. God is present and desires that we know him in all his fullness. That is why we practice God's presence, because God wants us to know that nearness and that love. Take some time now to totally relax and trust God to fill you with joy and love in ways that you can feel and savor."
  (Pause 30 seconds.)
  "As you continue to experience God's presence, listen to the 91st Psalm."
  (Read Psalm 91 slowly. End with one minute of silence. Conclude with:)
  "When you feel ready, open your eyes and come back to this place. Take your time."
  (Allow a moment or two for the class members to re-orient themselves.)

Closing

  May every experience of your day be an experience of Jesus. May you see God's presence in everyone you meet. May you see God's hand in every encounter of your day. May every person, every smile, every tear, every experience of God's creation be a reminder of God's presence and love. Amen.

CHAPTER-MODULE 4

Why Care?

Goals

Participants may:

4-A Display a stronger sense of identity as distinctively Christian caregivers.

4-B Learn when it is probably inappropriate to share their Christian motivation.

4-C Explore together the variety of motivations for caring.

4-D Understand better their ultimate reason for: (a) being a Christian, and (b) giving Christian care.

4-E Experience their own need for Jesus' help in complete caring.

4-F Experience Christian community.

Opening Prayer

Our Lord and God, because you reach out to us in love, we are able to touch others with the power of your love. Continue to mold and shape us into dispensers of that love in our community. Give us the strength to continue sharing your love and mercy even when the road becomes difficult. Not even death could stop you from loving us. Give us the same determination and power, for the sake of your Son Jesus. Amen.

Lead-In

Why do you do what you do? This is an important question. It is especially important that all of us ask this question of ourselves as Christians who seek ways to share God's love and concern in the world. This chapter-module will help us to explore how we answer this vital "why" question. This in turn should give us a better understanding of how God enables us to be Christian caregivers and how solidly we are dependent on God for motivation and help. As Harry Emerson Fosdick points out in his book *The Meaning of Prayer*, we will always be at least partly unsuccessful in practicing our Christianity if we do not center our life on Jesus Christ. If being true to our Lord's summoning is not our dominant desire in life, we are likely to set it aside for other desires.

As we work through this chapter-module, keep in mind that the author of *Christian Caregiving—a Way of Life* has reached one place in identifying his basic motivation, but you might not be in that same place. But you can get to a fully dedicated life of service to God and your fellow human beings if you want to! This does not mean that it is quick or easy, but only that it is possible, with real effort. Consider the prayer of Jeremy Taylor, a 17th century English believer: "O Eternal God, sanctify my body and soul, my thoughts and my intentions, my words and my actions, that whatsoever I shall think, or speak, or do, may be by me designed for the glorification of your name, and by your blessing, it may be effective and successful in the work of God."

Discussion Questions

A. Why do you, as a Christian, care? (*4-B, 4-E*)
B. Look at the quote from Carl Jung on page 32 of *Christian Caregiving—a Way of Life* where he asserts that all his patients' emotional struggles in the second half of life result from having "lost that which the living religions of every age have given to their followers." What implication does this have for you as a caregiver? (*Discuss briefly. Then ask:*) For the person receiving your care? (*4-D*)
C. Think of a recent situation in which you were called on to care. What was satisfactory about the interaction? (*Discuss. Then ask:*) What was unsatisfactory? (*4-C, 4-D*)

D. In the situation you described in C above, how did the "solid foundation" of your Christian behavior—"identity," "humility," "assurance," and "perspective" (*Christian Caregiving—a Way of Life*, p. 36)—influence or fail to influence your interaction? (*4-E*)
E. Does your underlying motivation have anything to say about possible feelings of frustration you experience in your caring? (*4-A, 4-C*)
F. How do we gain the right to share our *Christian* motivation for caring? (*4-B, 4-C*)

Experiential Learning Exercises

Note to Leader: It is highly desirable to use this first exercise because it continues the process of relationship and trust building in a nonthreatening way.

1. Why I Do What I Do (4-F)

Time: 8-10 minutes
Grouping: Pairs

Leader: *Read the following instructions:*
"In the next few minutes, tell your partner about your present vocation or task in life and why you do it. I'll let you know when you should change from talker to listener. You'll have about four minutes each. Go ahead."
(*Inform the pairs when four minutes have elapsed, so they can reverse roles, and when they have 30 seconds left overall.*)

2. Why I Am Who I Am (4-A, 4-F)

Time: 8-10 minutes
Grouping: Pairs

Leader: *Read the following instructions:*
"In the next 10 minutes, share with your partner the reason(s) why you are a Christian."
(*Inform the pairs when half the time has elapsed, and when there are 30 seconds left overall.*)

3. The Old, Old Story (4-D, 4-E)

Time: 25 minutes
Grouping: Individual at first, then groups of three
Materials: Paper, pen or pencil for each participant

Leader: *Read the following:*
"Work alone for the next few minutes. Write the story of Jesus from your own perspective, focusing on how that story communicates to you the reasons why we Christians love and care. Go ahead."

(Inform the class when six or seven minutes have elapsed. After eight minutes, have participants form groups of three. Then say:)
"Now choose a convener in each group."

(When all groups have a convener, say:)
"Now share your story in your group. You may talk about each story after it has been shared, or share all three, then discuss them, which ever you would like to do. Let's take about 12 minutes for this. You can begin now."

(Inform the groups at four-minute intervals so they can shift roles. At the end of the exercise, you might want to take a few minutes to discuss with the whole group, perhaps developing a list of key points from participants' stories.)

4. Making a List, Checking It Twice (4-C)

Time: 30 minutes
Grouping: Groups of five
Materials: Recorder needs paper and pen or pencil

Leader: *Ask the class to gather in groups of five. Have each group select a recorder whose primary function in this exercise is to take notes. Then read the following:*
"In your groups, you are going to do some brainstorming. The key to brainstorming is that everyone throws ideas out as quickly as possible, without evaluating them at all. In fact, discussing or criticizing ideas is not allowed during the brainstorming session. The recorder needs to write down every idea the group comes up with. We will discuss them later. Any questions on how brainstorming works?"

(Answer any questions that arise. When everyone is clear about the process of brainstorming, read the following.)

"Each of you come up with a list of every motivation you can think of for helping another person; brainstorm any and all reasons you can think of why anybody might want to help somebody else. Remember, don't discuss or evaluate now. Just get as many as possible down on paper. We'll take about five minutes for this. I'll tell you when the time is up. Ready? Go."

(After five minutes, say:)

"Now go over your list and, as a group, mark each idea you have with one of three symbols."

(Write the following for them to see.)

S = Mostly selfish
U = Mostly unselfish
B = Both selfish and unselfish

"If a motive seems to be mostly selfish, mark it with an S. Write the letter S right on your paper. If the motive seems mostly unselfish or altruistic, write a letter U next to the motive. If it seems to have elements of both selfishness and unselfishness, mark it with a B. If everybody in the group can't agree on a marking, take a vote. We only want to take about five minutes for this so keep moving. I'll tell you when there's only a minute left. Go ahead."

(Inform the class after four minutes have elapsed. After five minutes, say:)

"Okay, please stop. Go through the same list of motives and make a second mark."

(Write the following on the chalkboard.)

H = Humanitarian
C = Christian
E = Either

(Continue by reading the following:)

"Put an H if the motive would most likely be characteristic of a humanitarian who did not believe in God. Put C if you think the motive would probably be purely Christian. Put an E if the motive would as likely be true of either. Any questions? We'll take five minutes, with a one-minute warning. Okay, begin."

(Inform the class when one minute remains. After five minutes, say:)

"Now, for the last part of this exercise, see if your groups can agree on the most important thing you learned from this exercise. When you agree on that one most important thing, have your recorder write it down. Then we'll all share these with the entire group. When the recorder is ready, look up at me so I'll know you're done. Any questions? Begin."

(When all the groups are finished, ask each recorder to read the group's answer.)

5. God with Us (4-C, 4-D, 4-E)

Time: 10 minutes
Grouping: Whole group

Leader: *Have the members of the groups get as comfortable as they can. Read the following very deliberately:*

"Close your eyes and relax. Use your imagination. Breathe deeply for a few seconds; get yourself calm and collected in any way that works for you."

(*Pause 10 seconds.*)

"Now think back to the last time you tried to provide care, to provide some sort of significant help to another. Let your mind go back to that time. What was happening? Think now of that period of time right before you made the decision to help, when you realized that the need for help was there, but before you had definitely decided what to do about it. Think back to your decision to provide the care. Try to remember what you were feeling, what you were thinking. I'm going to mention some motives most of us have, at least in part, when we decide to help another. I'll pause after each one. Examine yourself to see how the motive I mention might have played a part in your decision."

(*Pause five seconds.*)

"How about self-importance? To what extent did you help in order to puff yourself up? It sounds bad, but it is a very common human motive. How true is it for you?"

(*Pause 10 seconds.*)

"How about the deeper personal satisfaction a person gets when one helps another? How much of your motive was this?"

(*Pause 10 seconds.*)

"Sometimes we involve ourselves in helping others in order to avoid dealing with our own problems. How much of this motivation do you see in yourself?"

(*Pause 10 seconds.*)

"Sometimes we help out of sympathy, because we feel sorry for those in need. Was this partly your motive?"

(*Pause 10 seconds.*)

"How about specifically and distinctively Christian motivation? To what extent did your willingness to care for another stem from your realization of God's love for you? Does what God has done for you in Jesus Christ have something to do with your willingness and your ability to pass Christ's love on to your neighbor?"

(*Pause 10 seconds.*)

"Now, picture Jesus standing beside you. Try to feel his presence."

(*Pause 10 seconds.*)

"You may want to thank the Lord for what he has done for you. In your mind, respond to him in any way that seems appropriate."

(*Pause 60 seconds or so.*)

"Take a few moments, and open your eyes when you're ready."

(*Allow a moment for participants to collect themselves.*)

Closing

May our Lord give us the wisdom and the faith to experience deeply our motivation for caring. May our gracious God give us the openness to receive the help he wants to give us and pass it on as we have received it. May he give us the identity, humility, strength, and perspective to see that all of our lives, including our ability to serve others, are motivated and empowered by Jesus Christ. Amen.

CHAPTER-MODULE 5

Family Ties

Goals

Participants may:

5-A See one another as members of God's family and understand what that means for caring and relating.

5-B Experience the personal, particular functions of being members of the body of Christ.

5-C Grow in awareness and participate in the kind of in-depth relationships that Jesus modeled.

5-D Evaluate how well the congregation relates as a Christian family and ways to increase the overall level of caring.

5-E Experience Christian community.

Opening Prayer

God, you are present with us as our guiding parent. Out of your great love, you offered Jesus as our brother and joined us all together through your Holy Spirit. These family connections are essential to our lives. No matter what our own experiences in our own families, we know deep in our hearts what the ideal is, and we find it in you. Thank you, Lord. Enable us to receive the gift of love you so freely provide to us as your children. Help us to spread that love to all those around us. This we ask in the name of our brother Jesus. Amen.

Lead-In

We are encouraged to address God as our heavenly parent—even to call him *Abba*, the Aramaic word for "Daddy." This term shows how close God wants to be to us. God demonstrated this closeness dramatically by sending Jesus, *Emmanuel*, which means "God with us." Through Jesus, God shows us what it means to be in relationship with our Creator.

Jesus includes us all in God's family. He makes it clear that his understanding of family goes beyond blood relations. In Matthew 12, Jesus' mother and brothers came to speak with him while he was teaching the crowds. When he was told of their arrival, Jesus responded, "Who is my mother, and who are my brothers?" He then pointed to his disciples and said, "Here are my mother and my brothers! For whoever does the will of my Father in heaven is my brother and sister and mother" (Matthew 12:48-49). Our relation to God provides the foundation for our relationship to each other. It is a common bond through which we may interact and minister to each other in meaningful ways. The potential intimacy this connection provides is an important witness to all around us.

In this module, we will explore what it means to be part of God's family. We will look at our current relationships to discover the potential that God provides within each of them. We will also examine how our relationship with God can influence our relationships with others. In addition, we will evaluate the church's ways of functioning as a family.

Discussion Questions

A. How is the Christian church like a family? How is it different? (5-A)
B. What are some of the specific benefits and responsibilities that are ours as members of the Christian family? (5-B)
C. What guiding principles provide the basis for our care of one another? (5-A, 5-D)
D. Some people don't like *family* as a metaphor for the church because they think it smacks too much of a "closed circle." What would you say to that? (5-A)

E. What differences do you see between "prying into another's affairs" and providing Christian care for another person? (5-A, 5-C)
F. How does our Christian family membership give us a head start in our caring relationships to one another? Are there situations where our Christian family membership might hinder our caring relationships? (5-A)
G. If you needed to talk with someone about a personal problem, all other things being equal, would you rather talk to a Christian or someone not a part of the Christian community? Explain your reasoning. (5-B)

Experiential Learning Exercises

1. How We Are Alike (5-E)

Time: 25-30 minutes
Grouping: Pairs at first, then groups of six
Materials: Paper and pen or pencil for each pair
Advance Preparation: Write these directions on a chalkboard, overhead transparency, or flip chart. Conceal them until later in the exercise:
   1. **Share a couple of examples of what each pair had in common.**
   2. **What did you learn by listing your similarities as Christians? Are the similarities between Christians more or less extensive than the differences? More or less important?**
   3. **What implications do Christian similarities have for Christian caring?**

Leader: *Begin the exercise by saying:*
   "Stand up, mill around the room, and pair up with the person you know least. Each pair will need pen and paper. Scatter yourselves around the room and seat yourselves so that you can comfortably talk to each other."
   (*Allow time for participants to arrange themselves. Then continue:*)
   "I want each pair to come up with a list. It doesn't matter which of you does the writing, but I want both of you to contribute to making the list. The list is to include everything you can think of

that the two of you have in common. Confer together and come up with a list of how you two are alike. Any questions? You have six to eight minutes. Go ahead and begin."

(*Allow six to eight minutes. Inform the class when one minute remains. Then say:*)

"Okay, good. Now take five more minutes and come up with another list. This time, list the various things that you have in common because you are Christians. Ready? Begin."

(*Allow five minutes. Inform the class when 30 seconds remain. Then say:*)

"Fine. Now let's join together in groups of six—that is, three pairs put your chairs together into a circle. Then choose a convener."

(*Pause for this to happen. Then show the directions you have previously written and say:*)

"Come up with a *group* response to these three directions. Let's take about 15 minutes for this. Go ahead."

Note to Leader: The next exercise assumes that participants are members of the same congregation. Change or omit it if this assumption is not true.

2. How Are We as a Family? (5-D)

Time: 20 minutes
Grouping: Individual, then groups of five
Materials: Paper, pen or pencil
Advance Preparation: Draw the following on a chalkboard, flip chart, or overhead transparency:

No
Family
Feeling
at All
Total
Family
Feeling

0 1 2 3 4 5 6 7 8 9 10

In another area of the chalkboard, or on an additional flip chart page or transparency, write the following questions for later use in the exercise:

1. In what ways is our congregation, or part of it, good at being a family?
2. In what ways is it not so good?
3. How could we develop more in-depth relationships among ourselves as a congregation?

Leader: *Begin the exercise by saying:*

"Each of you reproduce this "Family Feeling Line" on a piece of paper."

(Pause. Wait for them to complete this task. Then go on:)

"Now think about our congregation. Where does it fall? How much family feeling is evident? Take about one minute to consider that, then put a mark on your line that shows your conclusion."

(At the end of a minute, ask participants to gather in groups of five. When groups are formed, say:)

"Now choose a convener who will serve as a recorder. He or she needs paper and a pen or pencil."

(Pause briefly. Then say:)

"Each small group will evaluate our congregation as a family. Share where each of you placed the congregation on your "Family Feeling Line." Then answer these questions." *(Reveal the questions you wrote previously, and go on:)* "Take 10 minutes to record your ideas and conclusions. Groups will then share with everyone."

(Inform the class when one minute remains. At the end of 10 minutes, ask each group to share briefly their conclusions. Say:)

"Let's take a few minutes to consider how to encourage a deeper sense of family in our congregation. What are some things we could do as a group to facilitate better relationships within our congregation?" *(Discuss. Then ask:)* "In what ways can we reach out to those outside our congregation to include them in our family?"

3. Giving and Receiving Help (5-A, 5-C, 5-E)

Time: 20 minutes

Grouping: Whole group at first, then groups of five

Advance Preparation: Write the following (but keep concealed) on a chalkboard, flip chart, or overhead transparency:

1. What did you experience in this exercise?
2. Why is help sometimes hard to accept?
3. What are the implications of this exercise regarding active caring for your neighbor?

Note to Leader: As in all guided meditations, it is important to give the class a chance to relax before you begin. It is also important to read slowly, pausing a couple of seconds between each sentence. Longer pauses will be noted.

Leader: *Begin the exercise by saying:*

"I'm going to ask you to imagine something, but first I'd like you to relax. Close your eyes. Slow down your breathing. Breathe deeply. Really relax."

(Pause 10 seconds.)

"Think of a time when you needed help, but were reluctant to ask for it. Get a specific incident in mind."

(Pause 15 seconds.)

"I want you to relive the incident in your imagination. What was the problem? Try to experience again what you felt at the time."

(Pause 10 seconds.)

"You must have thought about asking for help. Why didn't you? Try to experience again the feelings elicited by the thought of asking for help from others, the thought of accepting help."

(Pause 10 seconds.)

"Imagine how wonderful it would have been had someone broken through your reluctance and come to you instead of waiting for you to take the initiative. Think of how it would have felt to have someone listen to you . . . to have someone understand. Now, go back in your mind to another incident in your life, this time one in which someone *did* help you, where you were able to accept help. Think of that situation."

(Pause 15 seconds.)

"How did it feel?"

(Pause 10 seconds.)

"Now come back to the present. When you feel ready, slowly open your eyes."

(Wait until the group is attentive. Ask them to form groups of five. When they have done so, say:)

"Now choose a convener."

(Pause briefly. Then show them the questions you previously wrote, and say:)

"Working very quickly, come up with a group answer to each of these questions. Go ahead."

4. Jesus' Caring Ministry (5-C)

Time: 20-25 minutes
Grouping: Groups of five or six

Materials: A Bible for each participant, pen or pencil, and paper for each group
Advance Preparation: On a chalkboard, flip chart, or overhead transparency, write the following questions:
   1. In what ways did Jesus show compassion for the various people in this story?
   2. What does this passage teach us about the nature of Jesus' "family"?
   3. What implications can we draw from this narrative regarding how we can provide care to others?
   Also prepare slips of paper (as many as you will have groups), each with one of the following Scripture passages on it: Mark 6:30-44; John 4:5-30; John 13:1-20.

Leader: *Ask participants to form groups of five or six. Wait for them to get arranged. Then say:*
   "Now choose a convener, who will keep the group focused and moving, and a recorder, someone to write down your group's ideas."
   (*While groups are doing this, distribute Bibles to all, a pen or pencil and writing paper to the recorder, and one of your previously prepared slips of paper containing a Scripture passage to each convener. Then say:*)
   "Jesus provided care in many different ways throughout his ministry. We are going to look at just a few Scriptures that illustrate Jesus' caring ministry. Have one person in your group read aloud the passage you have been given, or read it together silently. Once you have read the passage, discuss the questions written here."
   (*Indicate your previously written questions and go on:*) "Have your recorder write down some of your reflections. You will have about fifteen minutes. Go ahead and begin."
   (*Inform the group when five minutes remain and again at one minute. Then say:*)
   "Let's come back together in our large group and share some of our thoughts and observations."

Closing

   May God our Father bless us in loving community as we seek to live as a family. May our brother Jesus enable us to share our love with our brothers and sisters. May the Holy Spirit, our guide and friend, lead us to grow in the faith necessary to continue to build God's family with love and care. Amen.

CHAPTER-MODULE 6

Move Over, Freud!

Goals

Participants may:

6-A Recognize and articulate the value of faith in caring for deep needs.

6-B Grow in understanding how faith resources and psychological insights work together.

6-C Work together on a theology of caring.

6-D Explore and deal with feelings of inadequacy as caregivers.

6-E Gain a deeper sense of how God meets deeply felt spiritual needs.

6-F Experience Christian community.

Opening Prayer

Thank you, God, for the gift of our faith. Sometimes we take it for granted. Enable us to remember its value in our lives. Allow us to use it to minister to others and affirm and value their worth. Help us to care for others as you care for them. May our caring ministry truly be ministry, in Jesus' name. Amen.

Lead-In

Paul tells us in Galatians to "Bear one another's burdens, and in this way you will fulfill the law of Christ" (Galatians 6:2). As Christians we seek the best ways in which to do this. We strive to provide meaningful and effective care for our brothers and sisters. Our faith tradition gives us many helpful resources for such caring ministry.

Secular psychology also offers resources that are useful in Christian caregiving, however. Typically we do not use these resources to their full potential. We may draw a sharp line between the secular and the spiritual. Such distinctions neglect God's presence in all of creation. God is able to work through all resources, secular and spiritual, when they are used to help others lead more abundant lives. As we seek to bear the burdens of others in Jesus' name, we can use the treasures of both the secular and spiritual with God's guidance.

In this session, we will explore the necessity of both spiritual and psychological resources. We will see how God meets the deep needs of people. We will also look at how God reaches out to us in our deepest need, as well as how God works through us to help meet the deep needs of others in pain.

Discussion Questions

A. In *Christian Caregiving—a Way of Life*, page 45, do you agree with the author's statement that "Christian caregiving is superior to caregiving of any other kind?" Why, or why not? (6-A)

B. What are the greatest gifts psychology can contribute to the task of caring for others? (6-B)

C. The author claims on page 45 that "Christian caregiving has significant advantages over any other method; the primary advantage is that of depth." What do you understand this to mean? (6-B, 6-E)

D. What does the Christian approach to caring offer secular psychology to help it realize its greatest potential? (6-A, 6-B)

E. According to the author, if we are to understand our identity and be truly competent, we must be well versed in our Christian field, just as secular caregivers are in theirs. What kind of "homework" do you think is necessary to be a competent *Christian* caregiver? (6-A)

F. What "polishing" has our congregation given us "Christian diamonds" already? (6-E)

G. What theology forms the basis for your Christian caring? Or— another way to ask the same question—which of your understandings of God serve as the source for your ability to be a Christian caregiver? (6-C)
H. When should someone be referred to a professional helper or agency? (6-B)

Experiential Learning Exercises

1. Putting It Together (6-A, 6-B, 6-C)

Time: 20 minutes
Grouping: Groups of five
Materials: Paper, pen or pencil (for recorders)

Leader: *Divide the class into groups of five. Wait until they have formed groups, and then say:*
"Each group should choose a recorder, who will write down all your ideas."
(*Pause briefly. Then read the following:*)
"Each group spend five minutes brainstorming as many answers as possible to the question, 'What has God given us as Christians in particular that we can bring to our work of caring?' Have the recorder in your group write down all your ideas." (*Repeat the question. Then say:*) "Go ahead."
(*At the end of five minutes, say:*)
"Now spend five more minutes brainstorming answers to this question: 'What have I gained or could I gain from a better understanding of secular psychology to enhance my Christian caring?' Write down these ideas also." (*Repeat the question. Then say:*) "Go ahead."
(*At the end of five minutes, discuss with the whole group their answers to each question. Make master lists on the chalkboard or flip chart. Then say:*)
"Using the insights we all just compiled, each group write a statement that summarizes the nature of Christian caregiving. You will have just five minutes. Go ahead and begin."
(*At the end of five minutes, with a one-minute warning, ask the groups to share their statements.*)

Note to Leader: If you use the following exercise, this would be a good place to insert another reminder about the importance of maintaining confidentiality in the group.

2. How Deep Is Deep? (6-E, 6-F)

Time: 10-12 minutes
Grouping: Pairs

Leader: *Ask the class to gather in pairs. When the pairs are settled in place, read the following:*

"Each of you share with your partner your answer to this question: 'What is your deepest question or issue to which Christianity has spoken significantly or provided you a solution?' Share the issue and the solution. Take about five minutes for each. Go ahead."

(Inform the class at five-minute intervals.)

3. The Big Questions (6-E, 6-F)

Time: 20-25 minutes
Grouping: Groups of five
Materials: Paper, pen or pencil for recorder

Leader: *Have participants gather in groups of five. Wait until they have done so. Then say:*

"Now choose a convener."

(Pause briefly. Then say:)

"In the book *Christian Caregiving—a Way of Life* on page 45, the author says that Freudian issues are not very deep when compared to the basic questions and concerns of life, death, spirituality, and meaning. What are some basic questions of life, death, spirituality, and meaning? Spend five minutes in your group brainstorming and recording as many questions and concerns in these deep areas as you can. Go ahead and begin."

(At the end of five minutes, read the following:)

"As a group take 10 minutes to discuss how Christian faith has provided answers or insights to one or more of these questions for you. Each group should be prepared to share one issue and some possible answers or insights with the whole class."

(At the end of 10 minutes, ask each small group to share one question or concern along with the answers and insights they found in their faith.)

4. What Do I Need to Know? (6-D)

Time: 20-25 minutes
Grouping: Individual at first; then "interest groups"
Materials: Paper, pen or pencil

Leader: *Make sure everyone has paper and a pen or pencil. Then say:*
"Do you recall the author's statement on page 46 of the book where he said, 'Perhaps one reason why secular caregivers *seem to be* more competent in their areas is because they truly *are*'? He goes on to say, 'Christian caregivers—whether nonprofessional, semi-professional, or professional—must be well versed in their own area of expertise. Otherwise, the potential may be there, but it will never be realized.' This leads to the following question: What do you think you need to know more about to be a better caregiver? Write down one area where you wish you had more knowledge, more information, more training—whatever it would require to make you a better Christian caregiver. Take a couple of minutes or so to write it down. Then I'll ask you to share what you wrote."
(Give participants three to four minutes to think of something. Inform them when one minute remains. Then ask:)
"Who is willing to share what need he or she wrote down?"
(Whatever the volunteer shares, ask if anyone else had the same or a similar need. All who respond should group themselves with the first person who shared. Next, ask for someone else from among those left to read what he or she wrote. Form a second "special interest" group from others who share that need. Eventually you will have groups of two and more, plus a number of people with unique needs. Group all those together in a "miscellaneous" group. Then say:)
"Each group now take about 10 minutes to discuss ways you can meet your need. Each person select one action you can take or avenue of information you can explore in order to develop your area of need."
(Circulate among the groups while they meet. When appropriate, point out forthcoming chapters in Christian Caregiving—a Way of Life *that might address some of the educational concerns for some groups. Spend*

more of your time facilitating the "Miscellaneous" group, since they do not have a common need drawing them together. Inform them when one minute remains and then, at the end of the 10 minutes, ask for a report from each group. You might want to write these goals down as they are shared.)

5. The Secular and the Sacred (6-A, 6-B)

Time: 10-15 minutes
Grouping: Pairs

Leader: *Ask the group to gather in pairs. When the pairs are ready, read the following:*
    "Each of you take a minute now and think of a situation in which you received help from both Christians and non-Christians. Share your situations with each other and describe the assistance you received. Were there differences between the two perspectives? What were the strengths and the weaknesses of each? In what ways could the two viewpoints have worked together more effectively to provide a balanced response to your problem? Take about five to seven minutes each. Go ahead and begin."
    (Inform the group at five-minute intervals.)

Closing

    May God who created us so wonderfully give us the gift of understanding the tools of the caring professions. May God who died and rose for us give us the gift of faith to share with those we care for. May God who loves us give us the wisdom to use both these gifts in bringing healing to those who suffer. Amen.

CHAPTER-MODULE 7

Touching Spiritual Depths

Goals

Participants may:

7-A Display greater understanding of self and others in the group as people with deep spiritual needs.

7-B Understand and practice recognizing and relating to spiritual needs.

7-C Evaluate their personal relationship with God.

7-D Understand and practice ministry skills in the group.

7-E Experience Christian community.

Opening Prayer

Gracious and loving God, we look to you for guidance as we open our minds and our hearts to those in need. Teach us to care for our brothers and sisters who are hurting. Help us to find hurt where it exists and comfort those whose pain goes beyond the physical, emotional, and social. Work within us during this time that we put into practice your teachings and equip us to do your bidding. In Jesus' name we pray. Amen.

Lead-In

God has created persons to be multifaceted by nature. We are physical, emotional, mental, social, and spiritual beings. The spiritual dimension, possibly the most difficult to give expression to, is the focal one for the Christian caregiver, which explains why an entire module is devoted to concentrating fully on this spiritual dimension.

As we seek to understand spiritual needs more fully, both in ourselves and others, listen to Paul's words in 2 Corinthians 4:6.

> For it is the God who said, "Let light shine out of darkness," who has shone in our hearts to give the light of the knowledge of the glory of God in the face of Jesus Christ.

God has given us the cure for our spiritual needs through Jesus. As caregivers we will learn and practice skills for relating to others' deep spiritual needs. With God's help we may then possess the talent and understanding to reach out and help others who have spiritual needs and hurts.

Discussion Questions

A. The author claims that part of being a Christian is being a spiritual care provider. How did we Christians get that role? (7-D)
B. Why is it often difficult to talk about spiritual issues and needs, or perhaps even to think about them? (7-A)
C. A friend responds in a conversation, "I'm just so sick of all this talk about God." What kind of spiritual need might your friend be expressing? How might you "open the door" for spiritual talk? (7-B)
D. Because you know it takes time to truly deal with another's spiritual concerns, how might you deal with the following situation? Your friend has obviously been crying but responds that he or she is fine when asked, then breaks down and reveals that so many things are going wrong that he or she can no longer see God working in his or her life. You've got children or a spouse to be picked up and two meetings that evening, or some other pressing commitment. What might you do? (7-D)
E. What do you think about the assertion on page 53 of *Christian Caregiving—a Way of Life*, that our society, in general, is spiritually impoverished? (7-B)

F. Give some examples of how spiritual issues are important in the "Monday-to-Saturday world." (7-B, 7-C)
G. Can you remember an instance in which you wanted to bring up the subject of a spiritual need you yourself were having as you were talking with someone—but you didn't? What stopped you? (7-A)
H. Can you remember an instance in which you felt someone wanted to discuss a spiritual need with you—but didn't? What could you have said to encourage the discussion? (7-A, 7-B)

Experiential Learning Exercises

Note to Leader: Remind participants that everything they learn about each other is, of course, confidential.

1. Role Play Ministry (7-D)

Time: 30-35 minutes
Grouping: Groups of three

Leader: *Ask the class to gather in groups of three. After that, have them designate the individuals in the group as A, B, and C. Wait for this to happen. Then say:*
    "Now choose a convener in your group, who will lead the discussions."
    (Pause briefly. Then continue:)
    "We are going to do some role playing to learn more about ministering to spiritual needs. In each of the three situations, two people will be playing roles, and the third will observe. After each interaction, there will be a time for you to discuss what went on. After each person shares his or her opinion of the interaction, the three of you discuss what was done well and how the helping could have been more effective. Remember, you don't have to be perfect.
    "In this situation, A and B role-play; C observes. Here is the situation. "A, a member of your family you loved very much has recently died and you are talking about the funeral, which took place yesterday. B, you care for A. As you do this, encourage A to open up about spiritual issues. You have five minutes. Go ahead."

(At the end of five minutes, tell the groups to discuss for another five minutes. Review the discussion procedure mentioned above. After the discussion, say:)

"In the next situation, *A* is the observer and *B* and *C* role-play. Here is the situation.

"*B*, you have been feeling very depressed recently and you are telling *C* about this. *C*, you care for *B* and try to explore the spiritual dimensions of this problem by asking open-ended questions. You have five minutes. Go ahead."

(At the end of five minutes, instruct the groups to discuss for five more minutes. After the discussion time, say:)

"In this final situation, *A* and *C* role-play and *B* observes. Here is the situation.

"*C*, you are having doubts about your relationship with God, telling *A* that the warmth and closeness of that relationship has disappeared. *A*, you are to help *C* look more deeply at this situation and to explore different aspects of it. You have five minutes. Go ahead."

(At the end of five minutes, have the groups discuss for five minutes.)

2. Once When I Was in Need (7-A, 7-E)

Time: 10-15 minutes

Grouping: Pairs

Advance Preparation: Write for all to see:

1. What was the need?
2. Were you ministered to in this need by God? By other people?
3. If so, did this ministry help? State how it helped, or why it did not.
4. If you were not ministered to, what ministry do you wish you had received?

Leader: *Have the class break up into pairs and settle around the room. Wait until this happens. Then say:*

"Share with your partner a time when you experienced a deep spiritual need. As you describe this need, try to answer the following four questions."

(Refer to the questions and read them aloud.)

"Each of you take five minutes to talk about your spiritual need on the basis of these four questions. Remember, it is all right to pass if you want to."

(Give a five-minute interval warning, and a one-minute warning. At the end of 10 minutes, say:)

"To close your time together, say a prayer. If your partner did not receive the ministry he or she needed, there may be a way in which you can supply part of that by means of prayer. Give it a try."

3. Dear God, . . . (7-C)

Time: 10-15 minutes
Grouping: Individual
Materials: Paper, pen or pencil
Advance Preparation: Write the following items for all to see:
1. In what ways is your relationship with God solid?
2. In what ways do you wish your relationship with God was stronger?
3. What is your most pressing spiritual need right now?

Leader: *Ask the class members to find a private spot where they can comfortably write. Wait until they have done so. Then say:*

"Write a private letter to God. You won't be sharing this in the group. In this letter include the answers to these three questions."

(Point out what you've written and read it aloud. Then say:)

"Take about 10 minutes to write your letter. Go ahead."

(After 10 minutes or so, ask the participants to spend the next few minutes alone in silent prayer—bringing their letter to God and listening to what God might have to say.)

Note to Leader: Be alert for individuals who might especially need someone to listen to them or otherwise minister to them during or after this prayer time.

4. Reading between the Lines (7-B, 7-D)

Time: 20 minutes
Grouping: Groups of four
Materials: Pen or pencil, paper for recorders
Advance Preparation: Write these thought-provokers on a flip chart, chalkboard, or transparency. Keep them concealed:
1. What clues might one send out, revealing deep spiritual needs?

2. A friend brings up several problems during a visit with you. You sense an underlying deep spiritual need. How might you use open-ended questions to encourage your friend to examine spiritual needs?
3. List ways in which spiritual needs are masked by other needs a person may exhibit.

Leader: *Divide the class into groups of four. Wait for this to happen. Then instruct groups to choose a recorder. Pause briefly. Then say:*
"Spend five minutes brainstorming each of the following thought-provokers."
(Reveal your first thought-provoker and say:)
"Recorders, write down all your group's ideas. Go ahead."
(After five minutes, say:)
"Now spend five minutes brainstorming answers to this next situation."
(Reveal the second thought-provoker and say:)
"Recorders, remember to write down all ideas so that we can share them later. Go ahead."
(At the end of five minutes, say:)
"Spend five more minutes brainstorming ideas for this third thought-provoker."
(Reveal your third thought-provoker and say:)
"Be sure to write down all these ideas also. Go ahead."
(At the end of five minutes discuss answers and ideas each group came up with. End the sharing and discussion after five to ten minutes.)

Closing

May God, who sees our innermost longing and fears, and who knows our every need, give us a discerning eye for others that we may be God's arm of comfort, whispered word of peace, and support to those crying out: "God, where are you?" This we ask in Jesus' name. Amen.

Ministering to the Whole Person

Goals

Participants may:
8-A Experience together God's holistic care through others.
8-B Work together toward relationships with God and others that are characterized by wholeness.
8-C Gain understanding of and experience God's *shalom*.
8-D Practice holistic caring skills in the group.
8-E Experience Christian community.

Opening Prayer

Lord God, in your gift of salvation you have promised us healing, abundance of life, a relationship with you, and peace—wholeness. Thank you, Lord, for this wonderful gift. Help us to accept and experience the wholeness you offer. Let us sing your praises, not only for what you do for us, but also for what you permit and enable us to do for you as we realize the potential life holds when we live wholly as yours. Amen.

Lead-In

Shalom. Have you ever noticed that no matter how much you possess, something always seems to be missing? God's response to that frustrating human condition is to offer us wholeness. God's gift of wholeness to us means being cared for physically, emotionally, and spiritually. Jesus said, in John 12:44-46:

> Whoever believes in me believes not in me but in him who sent me. And whoever sees me sees him who sent me. I have come as light into the world, so that everyone who believes in me should not remain in the darkness.

Jesus came so that we can have a life that is full and whole. In the second half of John 10:10, Jesus said that he came so that we might have life and have it "over-abundantly." He calls us to experience that "over-abundant" life and to help others do the same.

In this module we will discuss and experience wholeness. We will look at ourselves and at possible physical, mental, and emotional roadblocks we unknowingly construct that keep us from accepting wholeness. Once we have a solid understanding in place, with God's help we will learn to share shalom, or minister holistically to others.

Discussion Questions

A. What do you understand "holism" to be? (*8-B, 8-C*)
B. What do you think about the Hebrew idea that all brokenness in our lives is the result of a broken relationship with God? (*8-B, 8-C*)
C. People who let physical needs and desires dominate their lives are fairly obvious. Can you describe someone who lets the intellectual part dominate? (*Discuss. Then ask:*) The social part? (*Discuss. Then ask:*) The emotional part? (*Discuss. Then ask:*) The spiritual part? (*8-A*)
D. Have you ever fallen into one of the "pitfalls in being holistic" (*Christian Caregiving—a Way of Life*, pp. 66-68) in your relating with someone? What happened to that relationship? (8-B)
E. Turn to the diagram of Maslow's hierarchy of needs (*Christian Caregiving—a Way of Life*, p. 69). List some specific needs that would fall under each category. (*Accept suggestions. Then ask:*) Do you see our Christianity satisfying needs in any category other than the fifth level? Can you see when it might not? (*8-A*)

74 Christian Caregiving—A Way of Life Leader's Guide _____

F. Is there anyone you know or have known who is or was a living example of one who experienced shalom? (*8-A*)
G. What characteristics—physical and emotional—might one who has experienced shalom exhibit? (*8-C*)

Experiential Learning Exercises

Note to Leader: **Remind participants that what they learn about each other in their groups is confidential.**

1. Wizard of Oz (8-D, 8-E)

Time: 20-25 minutes
Grouping: Individual at first, then groups of four
Materials: Paper, pen or pencil

Leader: *Read the following:*
"Each of you think of and list two needs you have in each of these five areas: physical, mental, emotional, social, and spiritual. (*Repeat the five areas.*) In five minutes or so, I'll ask you to share these needs in a small group. Go ahead."
(*Call time after four to five minutes and ask participants to gather in groups of four. Pause for this to be done. Then say:*)
"Now choose a convener for your group."
(*Pause briefly. Then say:*)
"Now take a minute each just to read your list of needs to your group. Others take careful note as to what each person says. Go ahead."
(*Inform the class when one minute remains. After four minutes have elapsed, say:*)
"Use whatever you have learned about each other to make a *temporary* gift to other group members. Take a few minutes and catalog for yourself what you have in your pockets, wallets, purses that might be an appropriate gift for each of your fellow group members. Pick a different gift for each. Go ahead."
(*After about two minutes, say:*)
"When you are ready, the convener may start, presenting a gift to the person on his or her left, then to each in turn. When the

convener has completed the circle, the next person goes. Tell each person what you are giving, and what need of his or hers you mean your gift to fill symbolically. Go ahead."

(*Call time after 10 to 12 minutes.*)

2. All of Me (8-A, 8-E)

Time: 25-30 minutes
Grouping: Groups of five

Leader: *Ask the class to gather in groups of five. Wait for this to be done. Then say:*

"Now choose a convener."

(*Pause briefly. Then say:*)

"Take about five minutes each to share two things with your group:

1. Examples of wholeness in your life.
2. Examples of brokenness in your life.

Remember, you can pass if you wish."

(*Inform the class at five-minute intervals. At the end of 25 minutes— less if groups all seem to be done—say:*)

"Conclude your time together with each individual praying briefly for greater wholeness in the lives of the others."

3. Beyond Hurts (8-C)

Time: 5-7 minutes
Grouping: Whole class

Leader: *Have the class get as comfortable as they can. Read the following and pause at appropriate points after sentences. Begin as follows:*

"Sit back, relax, and close your eyes. Pull your mind away from distractions and think about yourself." (*Pause.*) "Think now of a physical problem you have had or now have. It might be back pain, headaches, whatever. Get in touch with this problem. Remember the pain. Remember how it felt."

(*Pause 10 seconds.*)

"Now, think of an emotional struggle you have had, or are now experiencing. Allow your mind to return to the last time you suffered from it. Experience again this emotion, as much as you can."
(*Pause 10 seconds.*)
"Think of a spiritual problem you have had, or now have, perhaps lack of faith, an inability to feel Christ's love for you, or putting worldly things before your relationship with God. Whatever it is, dwell on it for a few seconds. Once again, experience it."
(*Pause 10 seconds.*)
"Now, take yourself back to the time of Jesus' ministry in Galilee. Place yourself in the crowd. Seeing him. Hearing him teach."
(*Pause 10 seconds.*)
"Feel the wind on your face; smell the fresh air. After he finishes his teaching, he approaches you. Jesus looks into your eyes and asks you, 'Do you want to be healed?' Reply to him."
(*Pause 10 seconds.*)
"Watch, feel, and listen as Jesus puts his hand on your head and says, 'You are healed. It is not your body, or your mind, or your soul that is healed. *You* are healed. You are whole.' Jesus smiles and goes to another person." (*Pause.*) "React now, to your healing. Feel your wholeness." (*Pause.*) "Jesus looks back at you. Respond to him in any way that feels appropriate."
(*Pause one minute. Then end the exercise by saying:*)
"When you feel ready, you can open your eyes. Take your time."

4. Strengths/Weaknesses (8-A, 8-D, 8-E)

Time: 10 minutes
Grouping: Pairs

Leader: *Ask the pairs to situate themselves around the room facing each other. Then say:*
"Each of you take about two minutes to tell your partner the things you do best. Go ahead."
(*Inform the class at two-minute intervals. At the end of four minutes, say:*)
"For the next four minutes, share with your partner those things you do worst. Each take two minutes. Go ahead."
(*Inform the class at two-minute intervals. Then say:*)

"Finally, close your time together with prayer for your partner, thanking God for your partner's strengths and weaknesses and for the overall wholeness God has given your partner. Go ahead."

5. What Would You Do If . . . ? (8-B)

Time: 20-25 minutes
Grouping: Groups of three or four
Advance Preparation: Write the following on a chalkboard, transparency, or newsprint: If a care receiver were to ask you to make a written outline of the steps one takes to achieve a life of wholeness, what would you write?

Leader: *Ask participants to divide into groups of three or four. Wait for this to happen. Then say:*
"Now choose a recorder to write down ideas as you develop them."
(Pause briefly. Then disclose the question they are to consider and say:)
"You'll have 10 to 12 minutes to discuss and come up with as many ideas as you can. Remember that quantity is what we're going for here. We'll sort through the ideas later. All ideas are acceptable— as a matter of fact often one idea will spur another, so do not be timid about voicing your ideas!"
(At the end of the 10-12 minutes call the whole group back together and say:)
"Now let's share one idea at a time from each group until we've constructed our written outline together."
(Write ideas on chalkboard or newsprint for all to see in an outline form.)

6. Biblically Based Wholeness (8-C)

Time: 15 minutes
Grouping: Individual, then whole class
Materials: Bibles for all
Advance Preparation: Write the following passages on the chalkboard or a flip chart:

Luke 1:46b-55	Acts 3:1-10
John 13:1-19	Philippians 4:10-13
John 14:27	

Note to Leader: You may wish to look up other Bible passages in order to have enough for your class.

Leader: *Distribute Bibles to those who need them. Assign each person a Bible passage from the above list and say:*

"These passages describe how God has shown holistic care for the persons in the passage. Read whichever ones you have time for and identify what needs God is fulfilling. You'll have about five minutes. Go ahead."

(*After five minutes, have volunteers share what they learned. List their differing responses on a flip chart or chalkboard. Then say:*)

"These are only a few of the examples of holistic care that are recorded in the Bible. Perhaps some of you have other examples you'd like to share?"

(*Discuss for another five minutes. At this point you might share some of your own favorites.*)

Closing

Shalom we live,
Shalom we share;
Lord, help us give holistic care.
As you have made our lives complete
Let us share with those we meet
The peace, the joy, the light, the love,
As you have shone from up above.

CHAPTER-MODULE 9

Servanthood vs. Servitude

Goals

Participants may:

9-A Explore the implications of God's call to be God's servants.

9-B Identify and share their own instances of servitude.

9-C Explore the implications of God's call to serve other human beings.

9-D Articulate the difference between servanthood and servitude.

9-E Experience the freedom to serve, which is Christ's gift.

9-F Experience Christian community.

Opening Prayer

Heavenly Father, we praise you for the greatness of your love in sending your Son among us to serve us and, by example, teach us. The love that moved him to serve with such humility and devotion humbles us all and reminds us how much we fall short of his example. Thank you for this opportunity to learn more about true servanthood. Help us serve both you and our neighbors with more loving, willing, and joyful hearts. Amen.

Lead-In

One of the great confessions the early church made about Jesus Christ was that he was a servant. Jesus said of himself, "For even the Son of Man did not come to be served, but to serve, and to give his life as a ransom for many" (Mark 10:45). Jesus demonstrated the freedom with which he served in John 13. There we read the beautiful words:

> Jesus knew that the Father had put all things under his power, and that he had come from God and was returning to God; so he got up from the meal, took off his outer clothing, and wrapped a towel around his waist. After that, he poured water into a basin, and began to wash his disciples' feet, drying them with the towel that was wrapped around him (John 13:3-5 NIV).

Jesus, knowing who he was—the Lord, creator and upholder of all creation—served. Similarly, if we know who we are in God— "perfectly free, lord of all, subject to none"—we are freed to serve.

Sometimes, however, we serve out of guilt, fear, and a half-hearted sense of obligation. This is servi*tude*, not servant*hood*. It is more harmful than helpful, both to ourselves and others.

John Timmerman described servitude another way in his book *The Way of Christian Living*. He calls someone locked in servitude a "do-gooder"—doing good things in the world out of a sense of obligation, duty, virtue. Servanthood he likens to "doing good in the name of the Lord." Timmerman says: "The fruit of goodness must be understood above all as 'doing the right thing.' Goodness has purpose and authority behind it."[1] Servanthood, then, is doing good with purpose and authority, obediently following the will of God.

In this module we will explore the choice between servant*hood*— real service that flows from a freedom—and servi*tude*, which is not real service, but behavior resulting from bondage to guilt and fear.

Discussion Questions

A. Review the Martin Luther quote regarding freedom and duty in *Christian Caregiving—a Way of Life*, page 71. How can a Christian be "free" and "dutiful" at the same time? (*9-A, 9-C*)
B. What clues can we look for in ourselves to determine whether we are acting out of servanthood or servitude in a given situation? (*9-D*)

---

1. Timmerman, John H. *The Way of Christian Living* (Grand Rapids, MI: William B. Eerdmans Publishing Company, 1987), p. 108.

C. How do we get the freedom to "go the extra mile"—to be willing to give ourselves to others as much as we can? (9-E)
D. On page 72 of *Christian Caregiving—a Way of Life*, the author says, "A primary reason Christians become entangled in the web of servitude is the fear of not pleasing God enough." Have you ever experienced this fear? (*Discuss. Then ask:*) What other problems might this fear cause in a person's life? (*Discuss. Then ask:*) What is God's answer to this fear? (9-D)
E. Have you ever found yourself in a trap of servitude in your relating with others? (*Discuss. Then ask:*) Which of the four "pitfalls" (pp. 73-80, *Christian Caregiving—a Way of Life*) is most difficult for you to avoid? (*Discuss. Then ask:*) How could you avoid that pitfall next time?
F. How do you distinguish between a care receiver's needs and his or her wants? (9-C)
G. On page 75 of *Christian Caregiving—a Way of Life*, the author says, "As you learn to recognize your brokenness and feel at home with it, you will be able to capitalize creatively on the imperfections in your life of caring. At these times God can be strong in your weakness." Can you give some examples of where God could be strong in your weakness? (9-A)

Experiential Learning Exercises

1. Slavery (9-A, 9-D)

Time: 12 minutes
Grouping: Pairs

Leader: *Divide the class into pairs. Say:*
"Each of you share with your partner a time in your life when you felt enslaved to your Christian calling rather than freed by it. Take five minutes or so for this."
(*Inform the class when 30 seconds remain. At the end of five minutes read the following:*)
"Now please take five more minutes or so to share why you felt this way and perhaps how you might have stopped feeling this way."

2. Grumbling Care (9-B)

Time: 10-12 minutes
Grouping: Pairs

Leader: *Read the following:*
"Pair off with someone you know fairly well. Pairs should scatter around the room and arrange your chairs so that you can comfortably talk to one another. (*Pause.*) Designate one of you as *A*, the other as *B*. (*Pause.*) Now think back to the last time you undertook a task begrudgingly. You might have been manipulated into it, or you *should* or *had* to do it. Can everyone think of such a situation? (*Pause.*) Now *A*, share the experience with *B*. Tell your partner what happened, but particularly relate how you *felt* about the task, and how you *performed* it. You have five minutes each. When *A* finishes, *B* may go ahead and share experiences with *A*. Go ahead."
(*After four minutes, say:*)
"If you haven't already done so, take about one minute and finish with *A*. Then go to *B*."
(*Finish the exercise after another five minutes, informing the class when one minute remains.*)

3. Manipulation (9-D)

Time: 10-12 minutes
Grouping: Pairs

Leader: *Divide the class into pairs. Wait for this to happen, then read the following:*
"Please share with your partner a time when you have been manipulated. Take two to three minutes each for this. Don't describe how you handled the situation yet—we'll do that a little later. Go ahead."
(*Inform the class when 30 seconds remain. At the end of five minutes, say:*)
"Now share how you dealt with this manipulation or, if you didn't deal with it, what the results of leaving the manipulation unconfronted were. Take five minutes for this."

4. Obligation or Opportunity (9-D)

Time: 15-20 minutes
Grouping: Groups of five
Materials: Pen or pencil and paper for each convener

Leader: *Ask the class to assemble into groups of five. Ask the groups to appoint a convener whose function in this exercise will be to take notes. Pause briefly for this to happen. Then read the following:*
"We are going to do some brainstorming. Throw out ideas as fast as you can, without worrying whether the ideas are good or bad. No discussing or criticizing of ideas during the brainstorming session itself. The convener will write down every idea the group comes up with. We will discuss them later. Any questions on how brainstorming works?"
(Answer any questions that arise. When everyone is clear about the process of brainstorming, read the following:)
"Okay, come up with a list of every adjective your group can think of to describe the type of care someone usually gives who is doing it out of obligation, someone who is doing something because they think they have to, not because they want to. Take five minutes and see how many adjectives you can come up with. Go ahead."
(Allow five minutes. Inform the class when 30 seconds remain.)
"Now, brainstorm another list of adjectives describing the type of care you would expect to find from someone who is doing it because he or she wants to. You have five minutes. Go ahead."
(Allow five minutes. Inform the class when 30 seconds remain.)
"Take a look at the two lists. Compare them, then decide as a group the most important thing you've learned from this exercise. Take another five minutes. Go ahead."
(Inform the class when 30 seconds remain and then end the exercise. You may want to have the groups share briefly the main things each of them learned.)

5. Show and Tell (9-B, 9-F)

Time: 10-15 minutes
Grouping: Groups of five or six

Leader: *Ask participants to gather in groups of five or six. When the participants are in groups, ask them to pick a convener. Wait until this has happened. Then say:*

"Each of you in turn act out for your group what your Christian call to serve feels like to you. Don't use words; this will all be done in pantomime. Remember, it's okay to say *I pass*. After everyone has shown, take a minute or two each to discuss what each pantomime meant. Go ahead."

6. Pinocchio/Person Imaging (9-A)

Time: 20 minutes
Grouping: Whole group

Note to Leader: As in all guided meditations, it's important to give the class a chance to relax before you begin. It's also important to read slowly and in measured tones, pausing briefly between each sentence. Longer pauses will be noted.

Leader: *Begin by saying:*

"I'd like you to take a few minutes to experience the feelings of servitude versus the feelings of heartfelt servanthood, using a childhood fairy-tale character as a vehicle. But first, I'd like you to relax. Get as comfortable as you can. Close your eyes. Inhale slowly and deeply through your nose. Exhale slowly through your mouth. Again, inhale slowly . . . and exhale.

"Now, I'd like you to imagine your mind as a flip chart, covered with the writing of all your thoughts."

(Pause 10 seconds.)

"Now, imagine flipping that sheet of newsprint over the back of the flip chart, so you can start this exercise with a clean sheet."

(Pause 10 seconds.)

"I'd like you to picture yourself as a marionette puppet like Pinocchio. Imagine that this 'puppet you' is being worked by a puppeteer named, not Geppetto, but Fear, or Obligation, or Duty.

"Now imagine the puppet you providing care to a bedfast relative who's crabby, demanding, and full of self-pity.

"How does the puppet you look while providing care? Imagine your movements.

"How does it feel to be providing care as a puppet? Experience all the feelings."

(*Pause 15 seconds.*)

"Now I want you to see the puppet strings and your puppeteer dissolve away as you turn into a real person, like Pinocchio did. See yourself as a person who willingly reaches out to that bedfast relative because you truly care. How does the real person who is you look to you?"

(*Pause 15 seconds.*)

"How does it *feel* to be giving care because you *want* to? Experience all the feelings."

(*Pause 10 seconds.*)

"Now, I'd like you to slowly come back to the present."

(*Pause 10 seconds.*)

"When you feel ready, slowly open your eyes."

(*Wait until the group is attentive. Then ask them the following questions, writing responses on newsprint or chalkboard.*)

1. When you were a puppet initially, how did you look while providing care?
2. How did you feel as a puppet?
3. Who was actually in charge?
4. Could you truly help?
5. What feelings did you have toward your puppeteer?
6. How did you feel as you changed from a puppet caregiver to a caregiving person?
7. What did the "caregiver you" look like?
8. How did you feel as a willing servant?

Closing

Servanthood is God's gift and it frees from the bondage of servitude. Fellow Christians, know you are lords of all and subject to none, and knowing that, be free to serve all! Amen.

CHAPTER-MODULE 10

A Surprise Gift: Forgiveness

Goals

Participants may:

10-A Experience the freeing power of God's forgiveness.

10-B Experience together how the gift of forgiveness can affect themselves and others.

10-C Recognize themselves and one another as wounded healers.

10-D Practice caring skills in forgiveness in the group.

10-E Experience forgiveness in the context of Christian community.

Opening Prayer

O Lord God, too often we offer judgment and self-righteousness when we should exemplify forgiveness and acceptance to those who feel far away from your love. Help us bask in the forgiveness of your loving Spirit. Then empower us to radiate your forgiveness into all the corners of our world. Amen.

Lead-In

In the Gospel of John, Jesus appeared to his disciples after his resurrection and gave them the gift of the Holy Spirit, saying, "If you forgive the sins of any, they are forgiven them; if you retain the sins of any, they are retained" (John 20:23). Jesus has given us a heavy but wonderful responsibility: We are to bring his gift of forgiveness to the world.

Therapist, professor, and author Beverly Flanigan says in her book *Forgiving the Unforgivable:*

> Forgiveness is one of the only forms of freedom that any person
> can give to another. It is one freeing art that anyone, regardless
> of race, age, or material well-being, can choose to give another
> while he, at the same time, returns freedom to his own life.[1]

We need to freely offer God's and our own forgiveness to anyone desiring it, regardless of our personal feelings. When we do so, we live out God's freeing forgiveness of our own sins. We must not, however, offer forgiveness prematurely before a person has had the opportunity for self-examination and growth.

In this module we will experience the gift of forgiveness, learn more about its freeing power, and practice how to share it appropriately.

Discussion Questions

A. What picture of forgiveness does Martin Luther King Jr.'s description, (*Christian Caregiving—a Way of Life*, p. 82) give you? (*Discuss. Then ask:*) How might this picture help someone to understand forgiveness? (*10-D*)
B. How can cheap grace hurt the care receiver while forgiveness serves to help him or her? (*10-B*)
C. Why is listening so important to forgiveness? (*10-D*)
D. How can a refusal to forgive harm the person needing forgiveness? (*Discuss. Then ask:*) How can that same refusal harm the person refusing to forgive? (*10-B*)
E. Distinguish between self-forgiveness and self-justification. (*10-A*)
F. What are the best Christian words of forgiveness you know? (*10-D*)

_____
1. Flanigan, Beverly. *Forgiving the Unforgivable* (New York: Macmillan Publishing Company, 1992), p. 257.

G. How have the wounds you yourself have experienced in the course of your life better prepared you to be a caregiver to others? (*10-C*)

Experiential Learning Exercises

Note to Leader: You may want to briefly remind class members again of the importance of confidentiality. You might find it helpful to model a response to either of the next two activities by sharing an experience of your own forgiveness. If so, keep it brief—two or three minutes at most.

1. Remembering Forgiveness (10-B, 10-E)

Time: 15-20 minutes
Grouping: Groups of five

Leader: *Ask the class to divide into groups of five. Wait until all are in a group. Then say:*
   "Each group should now select a convener."
   (*After a brief pause for this to take place, say:*)
   "Spend about 15 minutes sharing with each other your experiences of forgiveness. Each of you take a couple of minutes to share a time when receiving forgiveness was a special comfort to you. If you can't think of an example you are comfortable sharing, just say 'I pass.' When everyone has had a turn, the convener or someone in your group will lead the group in prayer, thanking God for the gift of forgiveness. Go ahead."
   (*Let the groups know when 14 minutes have elapsed so they can move on to the prayer if they have not begun already. Be ready to move the ending time forward if it looks like the groups have ended early or to extend the time somewhat if it looks like they're deeply involved and need more time.*)

2. Transforming Forgiveness (10-A, 10-E)

Time: 8 minutes
Grouping: Pairs

Leader: *Ask the class to divide into pairs around the room. When all have a partner, then say:*
   "Each of you share with your partner a time when forgiveness has transformed a relationship in which you have been involved or

one you know about. If you can't think of an example you are comfortable sharing, just say 'I pass.' You have eight minutes. Go ahead."

(Inform the class when four minutes have elapsed, and again when eight minutes have elapsed.)

3. Blocking Forgiveness (10-A, 10-D)

Time: 12-15 minutes
Grouping: Pairs
Advance Preparation: Write these questions out for all to see.
1. Why did forgiveness not take place in that situation?
2. How do you think the relationship would have turned out if forgiveness had occurred?
3. What would have made forgiveness possible?

Leader: *Have the class divide into pairs. Wait for this to happen. Then indicate the questions you have written in advance, and say:*

"Each of you share with your partner a time in your life when you were unable to forgive someone or someone was unable to forgive you. These questions will give you a starting place. Tell what this did to you, to the other person, and to the relationship. Take about five minutes apiece for this. Go ahead."

(Inform the class when half the time is up. At the end of eight to ten minutes, conduct a brief whole-class response to the questions you wrote.)

4. Wounded Healers' Radar (10-C)

Time: 20-25 minutes
Grouping: Groups of five

Leader: *Have the class break into groups of five. When everyone is in a group, say:*

"Now choose a convener for your group."

(Pause briefly. Then say:)

"We are all part of a broken world. It's been said that when some people have experienced an emotional or physical pain or wound, they grow an invisible pair of sensitive 'antennae' that tune in when they come in contact with others in pain. Share with your group how you got your own antennae and how they have become a source of early warning of the need for healing for others. If you haven't had this experience, describe a situation where someone else's antennae sought you out and you were healed. You have 20 minutes. Go ahead."

(Inform the class when 15 minutes have elapsed. At the end of 20 minutes, say:)

"Close with a sentence prayer from each person in the group affirming the others as wounded healers."

5. Bible Search (10-D)

Time: 20 minutes
Grouping: Individual, then whole group
Materials: Bible, pen or pencil, and paper for each individual

Leader: *Read the following:*
"For the next 15 minutes search through the Bible and find as many passages dealing with forgiveness as you can. Go ahead."

Note to Leader: **Some participants may be sufficiently familiar with the Bible to do this exercise without help. Others, however, might not have sufficient familiarity. For them, you may want to do one or more of the following:**

1. **Suggest that they look through Chapter 10 of *Christian Caregiving—a Way of Life* and note the passages there.**
2. **If their Bibles are cross-referenced, suggest that they use one of the passages in Chapter 10 of *Christian Caregiving—a Way of Life* as a starting point to locate others.**
3. **Encourage them to use a concordance to find more forgiveness passages. (You will need to provide concordances and may need to give quick instructions in their use.)**
4. **Use a concordance yourself to find a number of passages on forgiveness and list these for the class participants to look up in their Bibles.**

(After 15 minutes have elapsed, go to the chalkboard or newsprint and ask the participants to share the book, chapter, and verses of the passages they found. After you have listed everyone's contributions, urge the participants to fill in their lists with the passages they have missed. Suggest that this will be a good resource list for future study.)

Closing

May the freeing power of Christ's forgiving love fill us with joy, love, gratitude, and praise. May Jesus empower us to bring his freeing forgiveness to all we meet. Let us go in peace, carrying with us more loving and forgiving hearts. Amen.

CHAPTER-MODULE 11

Confession and Absolution over the Back Fence

Goals

Participants may:

11-A Get in touch with their own ideas and feelings about forgiveness.

11-B Add confession and absolution to their repertoire of Christian caring and relating skills.

11-C Reflect with other group members on the power of confession and absolution in their lives.

11-D Experience the gift of God's absolution from another Christian in the group.

11-E Experience Christian community.

Opening Prayer

Heavenly Father, thank you for the process of confession and absolution. Thank you for the freedom we have to tell you all, and the cleansing you offer in return. Help us to be more aware of this process in our own lives so that through our service to you we are able to share it with others who suffer the burdens of sin and guilt. Make us trustworthy. Use our time together now to strengthen, empower, and refresh us. Fill us, by your Holy Spirit, with the presence of your Son Jesus. Amen.

Lead-In

The primary emphasis of the first half of our study has been to provide a foundation of knowledge and confidence for you as caring persons. With this chapter-module we begin a greater emphasis on the practice and application of specific skills and resources available to us as part of our distinctively Christian calling.

Jesus breathed on his disciples and said, "Receive the Holy Spirit. If you forgive the sins of any, they are forgiven them; if you retain the sins of any, they are retained" (John 20:22-23). Sharing God's forgiveness is a great joy because you see God bring peace to the tear-streaked faces of burdened people. It is also a grave responsibility to determine if and when to share a message of forgiveness.

Let's spend some time now experiencing the joy and increasing our skills in learning if, when, and how to share God's forgiveness with others.

Discussion Questions

A. Can you give a description of Jesus' view of confession and absolution? Check out the following passages for some help with this question: Matt. 7:9-15; 18:21-35; Luke 7:40-48; 17:3-4. (11-A)
B. Do you agree with the author's position (*Christian Caregiving—a Way of Life*, p. 92) that you can announce God's forgiveness to another? Why, or why not? (11-A)
C. Can you envision a situation in which you would refuse to speak a word of forgiveness? If so, describe it. If not, why not? (11-A)
D. According to the author, what's wrong with "Harsh Harry's" approach to the confession and absolution process? (*Discuss. Then ask:*) What's wrong with "Libertine Larry's"? (*Discuss. Then ask:*) Have you ever found yourself in similar situations reacting in either of these ways? (11-B)
E. What does the author think is right about how "Caring Cary" handled the interaction? Do you agree? (*Discuss. Then ask:*) What specifically might you do to incorporate these behaviors into your caring? (11-B)

F. If a person decides just to confess to God privately and announce forgiveness to himself or herself, what might be missing? What makes including another person in the confession and absolution process worthwhile? *(11-C)*

1. Experiential Learning Exercises

1. Forgiveness Looks Like . . . (11-A, 11-E)

Time: 20 minutes
Grouping: Individual, then small groups of five
Materials: An assortment of paper, pens, pencils, crayons or colored pens, modeling clay, wire twisters, and any other medium you think the members of the class might use to express themselves creatively
Advance Preparation: Prepare some work areas with newspapers spread on tables for the messier forms of creativity.

Leader: *Indicate the materials you have provided and say:*
"We have several different media here that you can use in this project. Choose a creative medium and spend 10 minutes off by yourself using that medium to create your image of forgiveness. You can sculpt, draw, write poetry, write an essay: just let your creative self take over and somehow describe forgiveness. After 10 minutes or so, I will ask you to share what you came up with in a small group. Look over what's available to you and begin."
(Encourage the class to choose media and begin quickly. Be available to help those who are having trouble getting started. Tell them when they have three minutes left. At the end of 10 minutes, ask the class to gather in groups of five and share their creations. They should explain what their creations say about forgiveness. Allow approximately 10 minutes for sharing.)

2. Past Experience (11-B)

Time: 10 minutes
Grouping: Pairs

Leader: *Begin by saying:* "Pair up with someone, and the pairs should spread out around the room." *(Wait for this to happen. Then say:)*

"In the next 10 minutes, I would like each of you to share with your partner a time when you confessed to another individual or 'bared your soul' and 'got something off your chest.' You need not share the specifics of what was confessed if you'd prefer not to do so. Share how you felt before and after you confessed, and what the other person did that was helpful or not-so-helpful to you. Go ahead."

(*Inform the class at five-minute intervals.*)

3. "I've Got to Put This Garbage Somewhere . . ." (11-B)

Time: 10-15 minutes
Grouping: Groups of three

Leader: *Ask the group to divide into threes. Wait for this to happen, and then say:*

"We will be doing some role playing. Each group will need to pick one person to play the part of a caregiver, one the part of a care receiver, and one an observer. Go ahead and decide."

(*Pause until groups have decided. Then say:*)

"Here's the situation. The care receiver is suffering from deep guilt about something he or she has done. The care receivers need to imagine something to feel guilty about. (*Brief pause.*) If you are having trouble thinking of something, you can use this situation: Seven years ago, you took a sum of money from a place you used to work. You did it so skillfully that they never discovered the loss, and almost certainly never will. If you don't feel comfortable with this particular sin, construct your own. At any rate, I want you to approach the caregiver and try to ease your conscience in any way that seems appropriate. Got it, care receivers? You're in the mood for confession. I want the caregivers to help the care receivers to tell their story. One way you can do this is to listen without much interruption. If the care receivers are having trouble, encourage them to continue. When they are finished telling the facts, help them explore how they *feel* about what they have done. When you are positive that the care receivers have said everything they want to say, only then speak a word of forgiveness to the care receivers. Do both of you know what to do? (*Answer any questions.*) The observers should take notes on what they see. You have five minutes. Ready? Begin."

(*Allow five minutes. Inform the class when 30 seconds remain.*)

"The observers now share your thoughts and discuss these thoughts in your groups."

(*Conclude the exercise after five minutes of discussion.*)

4. Three Role Plays (11-D, 11-E)

Time: 30 minutes
Grouping: Groups of three
Advance Preparation: Write these questions on an overhead transparency, flip chart, or chalkboard:

1. **How did it feel, *A*, to have your confession dealt with in this way?**
2. **What needs of the driver were left unmet?**
3. **Why might the person hearing the confession deal with the confesser in this way?**

Conceal the questions until you are ready to use them.

Leader: *Have the class gather into groups of three. After all are in place, say:*

"You are going to do some role playing of confession and absolution. I am deliberately going to have you role-play two inappropriate ways to do this ministry and then one appropriate way. Please designate the people in your group as *A*, *B*, or *C*."

(*Pause briefly.*)

"Here is the situation for all three role plays. The person confessing was driving his or her car the day before yesterday and hit a young child on a bicycle. The child is alive, but in the hospital with cuts, bruises, and two broken bones. The driver had taken his or her attention off the road for a few seconds to wave to a friend. The driver feels guilty and believes the accident could have been avoided if he or she had been paying more attention. In this first role play, we will try the 'Libertine Larry' style. Remember in this style, you are to offer forgiveness as soon as you can. Don't allow the person confessing to express his or her feelings and guilt. In the first role play, *A* is the driver, *B* is 'Libertine Larry' or 'Linda,' and *C* observes. You have four minutes. Go ahead."

(*At the end of four minutes, say:*)

"Now discuss these questions for five minutes, with C leading the discussion in each group."

(*Indicate the questions you wrote in advance. Give a one-minute warning, and at the end of five minutes, say:*) "In the second role play, B is the driver, C is 'Harsh Harry' or 'Harriet,' and A is the observer. Remember, 'Harsh Harry' or 'Harriet' is the one who is heavy-handed, tries to make sure the driver is really sorry (according to Harry's or Harriet's strict definition), and neglects the driver's need to struggle and confess. Take four minutes for the role play."

(*At the end of the four minutes, ask the groups to discuss the same questions as after the first role play with A leading the discussion. Give them five minutes again, and then say:*)

"The third role play features 'Caring Cary' or 'Carolyn.' 'Cary' or 'Carolyn' is the one who listens, allows and encourages real confession, and gives the time for that confession to happen before offering God's real assurance of forgiveness. C is the driver, A is 'Cary' or 'Carolyn,' and B is the observer. You have four minutes."

(*At the end of four minutes, say:*)

"Now please take five minutes to discuss this question only, with B leading the discussion: How would this kind of confession and absolution be helpful spiritually? Emotionally?"

5. To Ask, or Not to Ask . . . (11-A, 11-B)

Time: 20 minutes
Grouping: Whole group, then individual
Materials: Paper, pen or pencil
Advance Preparation: Write these questions on a large pad of paper, a chalkboard, or an overhead transparency. Keep them concealed until after the imaging exercise.

1. What feelings did you have during this experience?
2. Why is it sometimes hard to confess sins?
3. What is it about this experience that will help you when caring for others?

Note to Leader: As in all guided meditations, it is important to let the class relax before you begin. It is also important to read slowly and in measured tones, pausing briefly between each sentence. Longer pauses and uneven tones will tend to interfere with the relaxation process.

Leader: *Begin the exercise by saying:*
"We are going to do a relaxation and imaging exercise. First, sit comfortably with your feet flat on the floor."
(Pause until they are ready. Then say:)
"Close your eyes, and slow down your breathing."
(Pause. Then tell them:)
"Take three deep breaths, release them slowly."
(Pause until they have finished this. Then say:)
"Think of a time when you committed a sin that you never confessed to anyone."
(Pause 10 seconds. Then say:)
"Think of the specific sin and the circumstances surrounding that incident. Try to experience again the thoughts and feelings you had during this time."
(Pause 10 seconds. Then say:)
"You might have thought about confessing to someone, but you didn't. Did anyone ask you what was wrong and offer help? If you didn't accept, think about why you didn't."
(Pause 10 seconds. Then say:)
"Think of another time when you committed a sin and confessed it. What did you say? What did you feel like when the other person listened to your confession, then offered you absolution?"
(Pause 10 seconds. Then say:)
"Now, when you are ready, slowly open your eyes."
(Wait until you have everyone's attention. Ask them to write their answers to the questions that you are about to reveal. Say:)
"Write your answers to these questions. No one but you will see these answers, and you can share them or not as you please. You have five minutes. Go ahead."
(Wait for five minutes, less if most have quit writing sooner, then read the first question and ask if anyone would like to share their answer. Proceed in the same manner with the other two questions.)

Closing

May our God give you the ability and the courage to care, to listen, and to share gentle acceptance and tough love. May our Creator fill you with the fullness of forgiveness so that you can effectively share that gift freely with others. Amen.

Tools of Your Trade: Their Use and Abuse

Goals

Participants may:
12-A State their understanding of the priesthood of all believers.
12-B Learn what many of the distinctively Christian resources are.
12-C See that there is a time to use distinctively Christian tools and a time not to.
12-D Share their faith and its practical resources with others in the group.
12-E Experience Christian community.

1. Opening Prayer

Lord God, you have made us your own—we are priests worthy to minister before you because of Jesus' substitutionary life and death for us. Truly you are a praiseworthy God. Equip us, your priesthood, with sensitivity to the needs and feelings of those around us, so that by using the right tool at the right time, we can be the gospel in the world and also bring your gospel to those in need. Amen.

Lead-In

God has freely given us a number of distinctively Christian tools to use when we care for others. Some of these tools include the Bible, prayer, and God's special indwelling presence. When we use these tools appropriately, they enable us to care and better communicate the distinctively Christian gospel to others.

In this chapter-module we will explore how to use distinctively Christian tools effectively and appropriately. We will gain a new and deeper understanding of our membership in the priesthood of all believers and our responsibility to others as members. We will also encounter God—and each other—in the fellowship of Christian community.

Discussion Questions

A. On pages 99-100 of *Christian Caregiving—a Way of Life*, Eric and Brenda responded inappropriately to someone in grief. How might the "tools of your trade" have been used appropriately to minister to the needs of the person described on page 99? (12-C)

B. What do you think about the author's statement that "You might determine that it is inappropriate to be overtly Christian . . . in some situations of human need" (*Christian Caregiving—a Way of Life*, p. 101)? Can you think of any situation like that? (12-C)

C. What are some examples of times when it might be appropriate to use distinctively Christian tools in your caring? (12-C)

D. What are some signs you might look for in the other individual to indicate that it is appropriate to use distinctively Christian tools in your caring and relating? (*Discuss. Then ask:*) What are some signs that might indicate it is inappropriate? (12-C)

E. What is the "universal priesthood of all believers" that the author refers to on page 101? If you didn't look at the biblical references listed there before, you might check them now. What does it mean for *you* to be part of this "universal priesthood"? (*Discuss. Then ask:*) How do you feel about this role? (12-A)

F. On page 104 of *Christian Caregiving—a Way of Life*, the author talks about treating people as objects when the caregiver is meeting his or her own needs, rather than the needs of the care receiver. Has this ever happened to you? Have you ever found yourself doing this? (*Discuss. Then ask:*) What specific steps can you take to keep this from happening? (12-D)

G. "The more you show your distinctiveness appropriately, genuinely, and effectively, the more other people will respect you for who you are and what you stand for—even if they do not believe as you do" (p. 104, *Christian Caregiving—a Way of Life*). What do you think about this? *(12-D)*

Experiential Learning Exercises

1. A Priestly Resumé (12-A, 12-E)

Time: 20 minutes
Grouping: Individual, then groups of five
Advance Preparation: Write for all to see on newsprint, an overhead transparency, or a chalkboard:

    Elements of a Resumé
- **Education**
- **Experiences**
- **Unique talents suitable to job**
- **Past successes**

Leader: *Refer them to what you have written and ask the class to spend five minutes writing a resumé of their experiences as if they were applying for a job as part of the Christian priesthood of all believers. Let them know that they will be sharing what they write with others. Tell them to be as complete as possible.*

After five minutes have elapsed, ask the class to gather in groups of five. Wait for this to happen. Then say:

"Now choose a convener, who will lead the discussion."

(Pause briefly. Then say:)

"Share and discuss each resumé. You have 15 minutes for this. Conveners, make sure everyone has a chance to contribute. Go ahead."

2. A Test of Application (12-D)

Time: 20 minutes
Grouping: Groups of four

Leader: *Ask the class to assemble into groups of four. Wait for this to happen, and then say:*

"Each one of you, taking turns, briefly present a situation (real or made-up) of emotional or spiritual need. After each presentation, the group should discuss which, if any, distinctively Christian tools would be appropriate to use. Try to state exactly how they would be used. Each situation and response should take about five minutes, so be as concise as possible."

(Inform the class of each five-minute interval as it passes.)

3. Learning What Our Christian "Tools" Are (12-B, 12-D)

Time: 20 minutes
Grouping: Groups of four, whole group
Materials: Paper, pen or pencil (for recorders)
Advance Preparation: Write these questions on a chalkboard, newsprint, or transparency, and keep them concealed:
1. **What tools (resources) has God given us that we can use in our work of caring?**
2. **What tools (spiritual gifts) do we have that God can use through us for our work of caring?**

Leader: *Divide the class into groups of four. Wait for this to happen. Then say:*
"Each group should choose a recorder who will keep track of the ideas you develop."
(Pause. Then say:)
"Each group spend five minutes brainstorming as many answers as possible to this question."
(Reveal the first question and say:) "Have the recorder in the group write down all your ideas."
(At the end of five minutes, say:)
"Now spend five more minutes brainstorming answers to this second question."
(Reveal the second question and say:)
"Have the recorder write down all these ideas also."
(At the end of five minutes get the whole group's attention and say:)
"Let's spend the next ten minutes discussing the answers each group came up with."
(Reread the first question and open discussion by asking the recorder from each group, one at a time, to read the answers. Entertain questions

and comments from the floor as the lists are read. Continue with the second question as with the first.)

Note to Leader: If you choose the following exercise, use it as a concluding exercise for this session.

4. A Time of Recommitment (12-A)

Time: Three minutes
Grouping: The whole class

Leader: *Read the following:*

"As we conclude this module, let's have a service of recommitment to our calling in the universal priesthood of all believers. Please rise and respond when appropriate. (*Pause.*)

"Do you understand that God has called all Christians, including you, to be his ministers at all times? If so, say 'I do.' (*Pause.*)

"Do you commit yourself to serve God as a member of the universal priesthood of all believers to the best of your ability? If so, say 'I do.' (*Pause.*) Amen."

Closing

May God draw us close to him and to each other through the promises of Scripture, the communication and closeness of prayer, the assurance and comfort of sharing him with each other, and the relief and joy of God's acceptance and forgiveness. May God so fill us with gifts that we are able to share them joyfully and competently. Amen.

CHAPTER-MODULE 13

Prayer

Goals

Participants may:
13-A Discuss together the what and the how of prayer.
13-B Deepen their relationships with one another by seeking God in prayer with other group members.
13-C Experience together the joys and difficulties of prayer.
13-D Become better able to pray with others.
13-E Experience Christian community in prayer.

Opening Prayer

Lord God, at your invitation we reach out to you, and you extend your hand to us. Teach us the confidence of small children who know how well they are loved. Be our inspiration as we lead others into the warmth of your presence. We see ourselves, hand-in-hand, daring to enter the throne-room of your majesty because we have been made royal ourselves. For this we thank you in the name of our friend and brother, Jesus. Amen.

Lead-In

Jesus models for us the necessity and the benefits of prayer. Frequently in the Gospels, Jesus is pictured as lifting up thanks to

God, drawing strength from God, and pulling away for a time in prayer. Clearly, prayer was essential for Jesus.

That view of God in the opening prayer may have struck you as a bit presumptuous, and yet this is the welcome we can expect according to Romans 8:15-17:

> For you did not receive a spirit of slavery . . . but . . . a spirit of adoption. When we cry "Abba! Father!" it is that very Spirit bearing witness with our spirit that we are children of God, . . . and joint heirs with Christ.

The word *Abba* is most truly translated as "Daddy." This is the intimacy to which we are invited.

It is an intimacy of Love, with a capital L. Martin Smith, in his book about praying with Scripture entitled *The Word Is Very Near You*, instructs us further. "Our prayer is not making conversation with God. It is joining the conversation that is already going on in God. It is being invited to participate in the relationships of intimacy between Father, Son and Holy Spirit."[1] Prayer for us is a high privilege; being allowed the honor of ushering someone else into that eternal dance of love is higher still.

Prayer is a valuable tool to use in our Christian caring, but it needs to be used sensitively. It needs to be accompanied with concern and by active listening.

In this module, we will learn more about prayer by discussing it and praying together. We will explore our own feelings about prayer. We will explore what intimacy with God and with each other can mean as we pray to him.

Discussion Questions

A. What is prayer? (*13-A*)
B. Many people find it difficult to pray publicly. What do you think are some reasons for that? (*13-A*)
C. How might praying with another person bring you closer to each other? What's special about that? Have you ever had such experiences with others? (*13-A, 13-B*)

_____

1. Smith, Martin L. *The Word Is Very Near You: A Guide to Praying with Scripture.* (Cambridge, MA: Cowley Publications, 1989), p. 28.

D. It's easy to *tell* people when to pray. It's often very difficult to figure out in a caring situation when is the right time. Have you ever been confronted with the decision to "pray or not to pray" with someone? How did it work out? (*Discuss. Then ask:*) What was good or not so good about it? How could it have been improved? (*Discuss. Then ask:*) What will you watch for in future situations? (13-A, 13-C)

E. What do you think about strongly expressing such feelings as anger, sadness, bitterness, and fear to God in prayer? (*13-C*)

F. Do you have a favorite prayer? What makes that prayer special to you? (*13-A, 13-D*)

G. What "language" of prayer is most comfortable for you? For example, how do you like to address God when you pray? (*13-A*)

Experiential Learning Exercises

1. Thin Prayers, Fat Prayers (13-B, 13-D)

Time: 15-20 minutes
Grouping: Pairs

Leader: *Have participants pair off with the person in the class they know least. Then read the following:*

"We'll be role-playing in this exercise, but we'll also be ministering to each other. First, say a prayer for each other out loud. Go ahead and take a couple of minutes to do this. Each of you in turn say a prayer for the other. Go ahead."

(*Entertain no questions or discussion at this point. What is important is to get them into the first part of the exercise without elaborating because that can ruin the main point. After each person has completed his or her prayer, say:*)

"Now each of you in turn share with your partner two worries and two joys that are going on with you right now. Let's take six to eight minutes for this. Go ahead."

(*Allow six to eight minutes. Inform the class when 30 seconds remain. Then say:*)

"Again, each of you say a prayer for the other."

(Again, entertain no questions or discussion at this point. A participant might say something like, "We already did." Reply matter-of-factly, "Just go ahead." The point is to have them do the second prayer without predis-cussion as to the rationale. After all have finished praying, discuss with the class as a whole. If it fits into the discussion, share with them the title of this exercise. You might begin the discussion with the following question.)

"What are your thoughts and feelings about what we just did?"

2. Private Prayer (13-C)

Time: 10-15 minutes
Grouping: Individual

Leader: *Although this exercise can certainly be conducted in your regular meeting place, you might want to have the class move to a church sanctuary, chapel, or other place where the quiet, the beauty, and the general atmosphere are conducive to reverent meditation, if one is available. Read the following:*

"In order to pray with others, it is good to be in the practice of praying privately. I would like each of you to spend 10 minutes alone praying. Pray for yourself and for others. Try to include praise and thanksgiving as well as requests. Just have a time of quiet com-munion with God and let God's presence be real to you. Your prayers are private and will not be shared with anyone."

(Inform the class when one minute remains. Gently break in after 10 minutes or so and have participants reassemble as a class, allowing time for individuals to complete their prayers.)

3. Praying Together? (13-A, 13-D)

Time: 10 minutes
Grouping: Pairs

Leader: *Ask the class to assemble in pairs. Wait until this has happened. Then say:*

"Each of you in turn share how you yourself feel about praying aloud with others. Discuss the pros and cons, the pluses and mi-nuses, the pleasures and pains, your possible fears, and whatever else occurs to you when you consider praying aloud with one or more others. Take about ten minutes to discuss this, first one sharing, then the other. I'll let you know when five minutes have elapsed so that each of you gets an equal chance to share. Go ahead."

(Give a five-minute signal, and also let the pairs know when about one minute remains.)

4. Remembering God's Presence (13-A)

Time: 10 minutes
Grouping: Pairs

Leader: *Ask the class to assemble into pairs. Wait until this has happened. Then say:*

"Each of you share with your partner a time you can remember when you felt close to God. If this experience included prayer, share how prayer might have enhanced or been part of the experience. If it did not include prayer, note if there were any possible ways in which the experience may have resembled prayer."

5. Building a Prayer (13-D)

Time: 15 minutes
Grouping: Groups of three

Leader: *Ask the class to gather in groups of three. Wait until this has happened. Then have them identify themselves as* A, B, *or* C *in their small group. When they have done this, tell them that* A *will be the caregiver,* B *will be the one receiving care, and* C *will be the observer. Then say:*

"On pages 114 and 115 the author talks about building a prayer, by which he means learning about the person and his or her situation before you launch into prayer. You C's or observers, you will be leading the small group discussion when this skill practice is complete. You who are the persons needing care, the B's in the group, I'd like you to take a moment right now to reflect on a place where you need prayer in your life. Make it a real concern, but one you are willing to share. While the B's are thinking, you who are the A's, the Christian caregivers, take this time to review pages 114 and 115 in your text and consider how you will proceed. I'll give you a minute or two now for reflection by the B's and review by the A's, and then I'll tell you when to continue. Go ahead."

(*After a couple of minutes, say:*)

"Now begin the process of building a prayer. Take about three to five minutes to build the prayer, and then conclude by actually praying with the other person. You'll have a total of eight to ten minutes, so be sure to actually get to the prayer. I'll let you know when you have three minutes remaining."

(*Give a time check after five minutes, and begin nudging people to close after eight minutes or so. Then say:*)

"Now discuss this among yourselves for a few minutes, with the C's, or observers, leading the discussion. What happened? See if you can develop a list of the *principles* for building a prayer."

(*If you have time, conduct a brief whole-class discussion, collecting the observations made in some of the groups, and perhaps listing the principles they derive.*)

6. A Prayer (13-B, 13-D, 13-E)

Time: 10 minutes
Grouping: Whole group standing together in a circle, joining hands

Note to Leader: **If you use this exercise, do it as the closing for this chapter-module.**

Leader: *Begin by saying:*

"We are going to have a corporate time of prayer. I'll begin the prayer, then there will be time for anyone else who would like to pray. Your adding a prayer is totally optional, but I hope if you are so inclined to pray, you will feel that this is a safe environment in which to do so. We will close by praying the Lord's Prayer together, and then I'll go right into the Closing."

Closing

May our God of intimate love bless us with a constant awareness of his presence. May God teach us to pray, both alone and with others. May God deepen our relationship with himself daily as we spend time sharing with him, loving him, and seeking his help and his will through prayer. Amen.

CHAPTER-MODULE 14

The Bible

Goals

Participants may:
14-A Deepen their understanding of the Bible's potential as a caring resource.
14-B Practice using the Bible as a tool for caring.
14-C Gain more familiarity with the content of the Scriptures.
14-D Learn to prize the Bible as God's Word to them.
14-E Discover other ways in which God communicates with them.
14-F Experience Christian community.

Opening Prayer

Blessed Lord, through your grace and inspiration you caused the Bible to be written. Guide us as we read it, learn from it, and hear you speak through it. Open our hearts to the peace and comfort to be found in your words, so that we may comfort others with those same holy words. Inspire us, O God, so that we may use your Holy Bible in a manner worthy of your great goodness. Watch over us today and bless our efforts to better understand and use your Word. We ask this through Christ our Lord. Amen.

Lead-In

We are a truly blessed people! God has given us such a wonderful gift—the Bible. Stop and think about it for a minute. God loves us so much that he gave us his Word. God's words were written down not only for our guidance, but also to comfort us during our struggles. That is the beauty of the Bible. It speaks the Word of God into the joys, problems, hurts, and pains of real people, people like us and those you love and care for. When we are in the midst of pain, we often forget that God is with us, *especially* during the hard times. The Bible serves as a wonderful reminder. That is why it is important to learn to use it well.

Like all tools for caring and relating, the Bible needs to be used with sensitivity and appropriateness. It will take practice. But with practice you will become skillful at not only introducing a Scripture passage into your conversation, but also matching the right passage to the right situation with the right person. That is what we will be doing in this session: starting to acquire these skills. Let's begin.

Discussion Questions

A. What examples can you think of from the Bible of God's strange and marvelous persistence in love (*Christian Caregiving—a Way of Life*, p. 118)? (*14-C, 14-D*)

B. Have there been times when the Bible has helped you in some difficult struggles? How did you use it then? What was most helpful? (*Discuss. Then ask:*) What was least helpful? (*14-A*)

C. In one of his writings, Saint Augustine has God saying to him, "What my Scriptures say, O man, I say." Do you agree with this statement? (*Discuss. Then ask:*) What practical applications does this statement have for your caregiving? (*14-A, 14-D*)

D. Have you any practical suggestions as to how we might become more familiar with the Bible in order to use it more effectively in our caring and relating? (*14-C*)

E. What are some advantages and disadvantages of using an older, traditional translation of the Bible in your caring? (*Discuss. Then ask:*) What are some advantages and disadvantages of using a newer translation of the Bible in your caring? (*14-D*)

F. In what other ways besides the Bible does God speak to us? (*14-E*)

Experiential Learning Exercises

1. Bible Favorites (14-C, 14-F)

Time: 15 minutes
Grouping: Individual, then groups of five
Materials: Each participant will need a Bible.

Leader: *Have the class assemble in groups of five. Wait until this has happened. After all are in place, say:*

"Working alone, please take several minutes to find at least two passages of Scripture that are meaningful for you. Be prepared to share their personal significance."

(After about three minutes have elapsed, say:)

"Taking turns, each person share *one* of your verses and its significance to you. If someone else happens to share your first choice before your turn, use the other verse you have selected. Or, if your first choice still has a very special meaning for you, share it anyway. Ready? You have ten minutes. Go ahead."

(Conclude after ten minutes have elapsed.)

Note to Leader: These Bible passages can be a rich resource for all participants. If you are not doing Experiential Exercise B, collect them in some way, perhaps grouping them under headings pertaining to specific situations (e.g., for loneliness or in the event of grief). Then you can distribute copies to all. Perhaps someone in the class would take on the job.

2. Applied Bible Passages (14-A, 14-C)

Time: 20 minutes
Grouping: Individual, then entire class
Materials: Bible, pen or pencil, and paper for each person; one or more Bible concordances
Advance Preparation: On a chalkboard or flip chart, write the following topic headings: Depression, Death, Grief, Loneliness, Illness, Forgiveness. Feel free to add more topics, if you wish.

Leader: *Begin by saying:*

"In this exercise we will be developing a resource list of Bible passages pertaining to specific situations for use in your caring ministry. You will be working alone at first, and then we will share our discoveries as a whole group.

"One of the tools available to aid your research is a Bible concordance. It's arranged much like a dictionary—you look up the word you're interested in, and if it occurs in the Bible, you will find a list of passages that contain that word. I have [a] concordance(s) here for your reference. "Now I am going to assign each of you a topic to research."

(Quickly go around the room and assign topics. When you have assigned them all, and there are still people left without topics, start at the beginning of the list and go around again. It doesn't matter if several people have the same topic. Then say:)

"For the next eight minutes, I want you to search for a couple of Scripture passages that you think would be comforting to people experiencing pain due to a situation relating to your topic. When you find one, write down the chapter and verse and place a bookmark in your Bible so you can find it easily, as you will be sharing these with the whole group a little later. Try to find at least two passages. I will tell you when two minutes remain. Let's get started."

(Inform the class when they have two minutes remaining. At the end of 8 minutes, say:)

"During the next ten minutes we will make our resource list. Choose one of the Scripture passages to share with the group. Please give me the topic, chapter, and verse, so I can write it down. Then read the passage aloud. We'll start on one side of the room and work our way around. All of you should write these down too, so that when we finish today we can each take home a good beginning resource list. If there is time, we will go around again for your second selections. If someone with the same topic as you read the passages you selected, just read us your second selection instead. Let's begin with you. . . ." *(Indicate someone to start.)*

Note to Leader: **It might help to appoint someone sitting near you as timekeeper for this last section, as you will be busy and could lose track of the time.**

3. Using the Bible as a Tool (14-B)

Time: 30 minutes
Grouping: Groups of three
Materials: One Bible per group

Leader: *Begin by saying:*
"For the next thirty minutes we are going to do some role playing. You need to get into groups of three. Let's do that right now."
(Pause for the class to get into groups. Then say:)
"We are going to do three rounds of practicing the skill of introducing a Scripture passage into a caring situation. Choose someone to be *A*, *B*, and *C* for each round."
(Pause briefly. Then say:)
"*A*, a year ago your teenager was killed in a car accident. You are in your living room talking with a church member who has come to care for you, to see how you are doing at the anniversary of your child's death. Your grief is deepened by regret over the argument you had with your child just before he or she died and the hurtful things you said. The thought that if you hadn't fought, your child wouldn't have been killed torments you; you're sad that your child's last image of you was so bad. You feel guilty, and the assurance you want most is that you are forgiven—by your child and by God.

"*B*, you are the visiting church member, and your job is to minister to *A* in this situation. A Scripture passage I would like to suggest is 2 Sam. 18:33, where David grieves over his son's death. Of course, if you can think of a more appropriate Scripture passage, by all means use it.

"*C*, you are to be the observer. Your job is to watch the action carefully in order to help the others answer the discussion questions.

"You will have five minutes to role-play before time is called. I will tell you when time is up. Take one minute now to get into your roles and look up the Scripture passage."
(Give the class a minute, then say:)
"Please begin your role play."
(After five minutes have elapsed, call time and say:)
"Now take the next three minutes to discuss your role play. Try to answer the following questions:"

Note to Leader: It will save time if you write the following questions on a chalkboard or flip chart during the first round of role play. Then you won't have to keep repeating them after every round.

"Was the *use* of this Scripture passage appropriate to the situation?

"Was its introduction into the conversation smooth and natural? Why? Why not? If not, what could have been done differently to make it go better?"

(*After three minutes or so, say:*)

"It is time to retry your role play. Switch roles, with B being the grieving parent, C the visiting church member, and A the observer. I'll tell you when your five minutes are up. Please begin."

(*After five minutes are up, call time and ask the groups to discuss the questions again. Give them three minutes. Then say:*)

"Switch roles one more time—C, you are the grieving parent; A, you are the visiting church friend; and B, you are the observer. Go ahead."

(*After five minutes are up, call time and ask the groups to discuss the questions. Conclude the discussion after three minutes.*)

4. Good News, Bad News (14-A, 14-B)

Time: 20 minutes
Grouping: Groups of four

Leader: *Ask the class to assemble in groups of four. Wait for this to happen. Then say:*

"I'd like each of you to take a few moments to think of a time when you saw Scripture used appropriately in caring, and therefore it was a blessing to someone. It can be a time when Scripture was shared with you or someone else. The important thing here is to identify *why* the use of Scripture was a blessing, so we can learn from it. Take about ten minutes. I'll tell you when time is up. You may begin."

(*After about 10 minutes have elapsed, say:*)

"Okay. Now let's take another ten minutes and do the opposite of the last exercise. Take a few moments to think of a caring situation

when you saw Scripture used inappropriately. Again, the important thing is to identify *why* it was inappropriate at that time. Go ahead."
   (*Conclude the exercise after 10 more minutes have elapsed.*)

5. God with Me (14-D, 14-E)

Time: 15-20 minutes
Grouping: Groups of four or five

Leader: *Ask participants to gather in groups of four or five. Wait for groups to form. Then say:*
   "Now choose a convener to lead the discussion in your group."
   (*Pause briefly. Then say:*)
   "Just as we communicate our love and concern for others in a variety of ways, so too does God communicate his love and concern for us. At times God speaks to us through the Bible. Other times it is through dreams, in prayer, or through other people and situations.
   "In this exercise, you are going to take a few moments to remember and then share a time when God really spoke to you, loud and clear, through the Bible. It can be a happy time or a painful time. What we are trying to get in touch with is God's loving communication with us through Scripture. As caregivers we need to be particularly sensitive to the fact that God communicates with us, since many times people in pain need a little assistance in hearing God speak.
   "You will each have about three minutes to share. I'll signal you at three-minute intervals so that everybody gets a chance to share. But first, take a minute to think about a time when God spoke to you through Scripture."
   (*Pause for a minute. This might be a good time for you to share a brief example from your own life, if you have one appropriate to share. Then say:*)
   "Begin sharing now."
   (*Inform the class at three-minute intervals. At the end of fifteen minutes or so, say:*)
   "Our time is up. Would everybody in your group please join hands. Take a minute now to mentally compose a one-line prayer of thanksgiving to God that he communicates with us through the wonderful gift of his Word."
   (*Pause for a minute. Then say:*)

"Now I want you to go around your circles and bless each other by saying your prayers aloud."

Closing

God speaks and things happen: People are
  confronted,
    challenged,
      healed,
        forgiven.
God speaks and things happen: People are
  helped,
    motivated,
      transformed,
        made whole.
God speaks:
  Let's celebrate!
  Amen.

CHAPTER-MODULE 15

Sharing a Blessing

Goals

Participants may:

15-A Proclaim God's control of their lives and the world through their use of blessings.

15-B Practice the skill of constructing a blessing.

15-C Gain familiarity with the variety of blessings available to Christian caregivers.

15-D Experience Christian community.

Opening Prayer

Dear Father in heaven, you love us beyond all measure and fill our lives with countless blessings. Bless our work here today and grant that we may now become channels for your blessings to those in need. Guide us as we learn to help others find the peace that comes from trusting in your love, through Christ our Lord. Amen.

Lead-In

Gesundheit! Have a nice day! *Adios!* Good-bye! How many times today did you say something like this? Probably at least a couple of times. But, have you ever really thought about what you were actually doing? You were sharing a blessing—secular or sacred.

In fact, we are all blessed. God blessed us when he created us. In the first chapter of Genesis it says, "So God created humankind in his image, in the image of God he created them, male and female he created them. God blessed them . . ." (Genesis 1:27-28).

Just as we've been blessed, so we must bless. Today we are going to learn to do just that!

The Exodus, the ark, Elijah and the prophets of Baal, the stilling of the storm, feeding 5,000 with almost no food, the death and resurrection of Jesus—all these events and many, many more are sources of strength and blessing to us. When we recall them, we are reassured of God's faithfulness, of his loving and wise rule in the world.

It is important for a caregiver to know how to share a blessing or benediction because frequently, when people are hurting, they need to know that God still cares and is with them in their struggle. Sharing a benediction is one way of linking a person with the whole history of God's saving acts. This knowledge can give individuals the strength they need to carry on. When used appropriately, a benediction is a powerful tool of Christian ministry.

In this module, we will discuss and study some of our favorite benedictions. We will learn to construct a benediction of our own, appropriate to the situation in which we find ourselves as caregivers, and we will practice sharing this benediction with others.

Discussion Questions

A. Has anyone ever given you the popular secular benediction, "Have a good day"? What were some of your feelings when this was said to you? (*Discuss. Then ask:*) Why did you feel that way? (*15-B*)

B. Think about some of the Christian benedictions people have given you, both in a formal (worship service, church, or similar) setting and in an informal setting (after talking with a friend, in passing, and so on). Which ones meant the most to you? (*Discuss. Then ask:*) What qualities made them special? (*15-C*)

C. How might hurting people be helped if they are reminded that their day is in the hands of God? (*Discuss. Then ask:*) What are the risks of so reminding them? (*15-A*)

D. Can you think of some examples of times when it might be appropriate to share a blessing other than at the end of your time with another person? (*15-A*)

E. Take a look at the "secular" blessings on page 123 of *Christian Caregiving—a Way of Life*. Can you revise these or some other everyday secular benedictions so they have a distinctively Christian flavor? For example, how might this be accomplished with "Have a good day"? (*Discuss. Then ask:*) What about others? (*15-B*)

F. On page 124 of *Christian Caregiving—a Way of Life* the author calls blessings a remembering tool. What acts of God do you recall that might have their place in a benediction you would create? (*15-A*)

G. Which Christian benediction is your favorite? When might you feel comfortable using it? (*15-B, 15-C*)

Experiential Learning Exercises

1. Experiencing a Benediction (15-A, 15-B, 15-C)

Time: 5 minutes
Grouping: Individual

Leader: *Begin by saying:*
    "We are going to do some creative imaging to get us in the right frame of mind to consider blessings."

Note to Leader: As in all guided meditations, it is important to give the class a chance to relax before you begin. It is also important to read slowly and in measured tones, pausing briefly between each sentence. Longer pauses will be noted.

(*Read the following in a measured, comfortable tone.*)
    "I'm going to ask you to imagine a situation, but first I'd like you to take a few minutes to relax and get comfortable. Close your eyes and begin to breathe slowly . . . deeply . . . rhythmically."
    (*Pause 10 seconds, then resume:*)
    "Now, I want you to remember back to a time when you *really* needed to hear a blessing. It doesn't have to be a time when you

actually heard one, just a time when it would have helped. Think back—try to get in touch with what was happening in your life. Were you ill? Hurting? Did you feel God's compassion or did you feel alone? Put yourself back in that situation."

(*Pause for 15 seconds, then resume:*)

"Picture yourself being ministered to and receiving a blessing. If you can't think of anyone from whom to receive the blessing, try picturing the caring, nurturing presence of Jesus ministering to you. What sort of blessing do you need to hear?"

(*Pause for 10 seconds, then resume:*)

"What is this person who is blessing you saying to you? How are they speaking the blessing? Do you want to be touched? When? Put in as many details as you can."

(*Pause for 10 seconds, then resume:*)

"When you feel ready, open your eyes and come back to the present. Take your time."

(*Wait until the class is attentive. Then say:*)

"This exercise helps you see and hear within your mind the way a blessing can be yours. Keep this experience in mind as we try other ways to gain skills in blessing one another."

Note to Leader: The following exercise is fundamental to the closing and should be one of the ones you choose. During participants' writing time, walk around the room and offer help to any who require it.

2. Building a Benediction (15-B, 15-D)

Time: 7-8 minutes
Grouping: Individual, then pairs
Materials: Pen or pencil and paper

Leader: *Ask the class to find comfortable places to think and write. Say:*

"For the next few minutes do some creative thinking. Construct a benediction of your own for someone you love. Recall the author's statement that blessings are a remembering tool. What acts of God do you want to invoke? You might wish to refer to Chapter 15 of the book for some help. Ready? Begin."

(Inform the class when one minute remains. Be sure to wait for everyone to finish up. Because of the nature of this exercise, everyone must be given time to finish.)

"Each of you find a partner now. *(Pause until all have found one.)* Share with your partner the benediction you have written. Remember the importance of touch."

(Have them hold onto the benedictions they have written for possible use in the closing. You might also want to collect and reproduce them for the group later on.)

3. Remembering a Blessing (15-A, 15-D)

Time: 15 minutes
Grouping: Groups of three or four

Leader: *Ask the class to gather in groups of three or four. After all are in place, say:*

"We have all received many blessings from God in our lives. But frequently we forget to count our blessings. In this exercise I want you to try to remember a time when God really blessed you. Then share that time with your small group. If you aren't able to think of a time, just say 'pass' when your turn comes. You'll have about six to eight minutes, and I'll tell you when only two minutes remain. Let's begin."

(Inform the class when two minutes remain. Then say:)

"Take the next six to eight minutes to remember and share a time you were given a particularly meaningful blessing or benediction. Again, if you can't think of a time, just say 'pass' when it is your turn. You can begin."

4. Situational Benedictions (15-B, 15-C)

Time: 20 minutes
Grouping: Individual, then groups of three or four
Materials: All need pen or pencil, paper, and Bible

Leader: *Begin by saying:*

"I want you to spend the next ten minutes alone, thinking about one or two people you know who are hurting or in some way in need of a benediction. Keeping in mind their particular situations, try to find appropriate blessings in the Bible or, if you prefer, write your own. You can write a blessing for one or both the people you have in mind, it is up to you. I will tell you when the time is up. Let's begin."

(*After the ten minutes have elapsed, ask the class to assemble in groups of three or four. When groups are in place, say:*)

"Now choose a convener for your group."

(*Pause briefly for this to occur. Then say:*)

"You are now going to share your benedictions with the others in your group. So that your benediction is more meaningful to the group, it would be helpful to share a little something about the person's situation beforehand. Please keep confidential any identifying information, however. After you have all shared one, if you still have time, you may share your second blessing. You have ten minutes. You can begin now."

(*Let the groups know when eight minutes have passed. Then conclude the exercise after ten minutes.*)

Closing

Ask the class to stand in a circle and bless each other by reading the benedictions they wrote for "Building a Benediction." (With a large class—more than 15—break into two or more roughly equal circles for this part of the closing, then come together as a whole for the final blessing.) After each person has shared, have the group speak in unison a loud "Amen!" When all who wish have finished their blessings, bless the group with the following:

May the Lord bless us and keep us;
May he give us strength to help bear another's burden;
May he give us patience so we can listen attentively;
May he give us healing words when we are called
    to speak; and
May his love shine through in everything we do. Amen.

CHAPTER-MODULE 16

A Cup of Cold Water

Goals

Participants may:
16-A Understand "cups of cold water" as Christian resources equal in worth to traditional resources.
16-B Understand the falsity of division between cups of cold water and traditional Christian resources.
16-C Experience a broader understanding of Christian care.
16-D Experience God's claim on their whole life.
16-E Learn some ways to give cups of cold water.
16-F Experience Christian community in the giving and receiving of cups of cold water.

Opening Prayer

Lord Jesus, your choice to become a vulnerable human being includes us in the completeness of your love. By suffering and dying in our place, you have encircled our lives with your loving arms. May our love for each other in acts of kindness be our tangible witness to your love for us. Amen.

Lead-In

In Matthew 25:35-36 Jesus' teaching about caring for others is plainly stated:

. . . for I was hungry and you gave me food, I was thirsty and you gave me something to drink, I was a stranger and you welcomed me, I was naked and you gave me clothing, I was sick and you took care of me, I was in prison and you visited me.

Jesus emphasized that reaching out in a practical, life-sustaining, and human way is vital in the caring process. Not only vital—it is reaching out to Jesus himself! These common courtesies—Jesus calls them "cups of cold water" in Matthew 10:42—become sacred because of the one we offer them to and because of the one who prompts our offering.

Answering all dimensions of a person's needs is important—both body and soul must be sustained together for the good or well being of the whole person. Keeping Jesus' direction for such inclusive care in mind, let's determine what makes an act of caring a Christian act of caring.

Discussion Questions

A. What would have been different for the author if he had just sat tight as the state trooper stated? (*Discuss. Then ask:*) What would have been different for the injured man? (*16-C*)
B. In *Christian Caregiving—a Way of Life*, the author asserts that "the distinction frequently drawn between sacred and secular is more destructive than beneficial" (p. 131). What do you think about that? (*16-D*)
C. What are some of the ways we "try to keep God boxed up and out of our everyday affairs" (p. 131)? (*16-B*)
D. The author writes that anyone who makes the distinction between cups of cold water and traditional, explicit resources an either/or proposition necessarily offers less than complete *Christian* care (p. 132). Which of these forms of caring is easier? (*Discuss. Then ask:*) Why might this be so? (*16-C*)
E. At what point does our caring become distinctively Christian? (*16-C, 16-D*)
F. God claims our whole life, both sacred and secular, as his own. How can this understanding change common perceptions of worship, church, stewardship, and the like? (*16-D*)

G. When have you given a "cup of cold water" to someone? How was that experience "Christian" for you? (*16-C, 16-D*)

Experiential Learning Exercises

Note to Leader: Do not announce the name of the exercise until the end.

1. Belling the Cat (16-A)

Time: 30-35 minutes
Grouping: Groups of five, then the class as a whole
Materials: Each group will need one pad and pen for the recorder.

Leader: *Have participants form groups of five. Wait until this has happened. Then say:*

"Now choose a convener who will also serve as a recorder. Recorders will need paper and a pen or pencil."

(*Pause briefly for groups to follow directions. Then say:*)

"Now I'm going to read Matthew 25:31-46 to you. Listen carefully because you're going to be doing some brainstorming later."

(*Read Matthew 25:31-46. Pause 5 seconds at the end. Then say:*)

"Now you're going to do some brainstorming. Remember, the key to brainstorming is to throw out ideas as fast as you can, without bothering about whether the ideas are good or bad. No discussing or criticizing of ideas during the brainstorming session! The recorders should write down every idea the groups come up with. We will discuss them later. Any questions on how brainstorming works?"

(*Answer any questions that arise. When everyone is clear about the process of brainstorming, say:*)

"The first list you're going to brainstorm is a list of human needs in our community. What needs do people have? Recorders, write down every human need your group can come up with in five minutes. Go ahead."

(*Inform the class when 30 seconds remain. After five minutes, say:*)

"Now brainstorm a list of concrete actions our congregation is taking to meet the human needs you named in your first list. Study groups and money that goes outside our own local community don't count. List *concrete* actions being taken to meet human needs *right here*. We'll take about five minutes."

(This list might take less than five minutes to generate. If it looks like the groups are finished early, move on.)

"The last list you'll do is a list of concrete actions that our congregation *could* take to meet some of the needs of our own community. Actions *our congregation* could take. Remember, you are brainstorming here, not criticizing or evaluating. You want any and all ideas. We'll evaluate them later. This list is important, so we'll take eight minutes. Go ahead."

(After 8 minutes, with a 45-second warning, have the various recorders read the results of their third list, "Actions That Could Be Taken." Collect these actions on chart paper or some other permanent record. Then tell the entire group the name of the activity: Belling the Cat. *Ask if anyone remembers that fable, and if so, ask the person to recount it briefly for the others. If no one recalls it, tell them the following:)*

"The mice were discussing an issue of grave concern: the cat. After much worried talk about what they could do, one mouse stood up and announced: 'I have it! When the cat's asleep, we will sneak up and tie a bell around its neck. Then we will always know where it is.' This solution was greeted with cheers, whistles, mutual congratulations, and a general feeling of relief until one of the old mice held up his paw for silence. 'This idea is all well and good, my friends, except for one detail. Who shall bell the cat?' One by one the mice stole away, none looking at the other.

"How does this fable relate to the exercise we just completed?"

(Elicit from the group or point out the notion that great ideas are plentiful, but it's their execution that matters. Lead an open discussion on the feasibility of the proposals. Make a point of saving the sheet with the "action ideas" on it.)

2. Fears (16-F)

Time: 10-12 minutes
Grouping: Pairs

Leader: *Have the class divide into pairs. Once all are in place, say:*

"Giving 'a cup of cold water' can sometimes be frightening. It can be risky for several reasons to offer help and comfort to someone who is injured, imprisoned, or trapped in painful circumstances.

"Spend six to eight minutes discussing any fears each of you might have about being a 'good Samaritan.' Try to determine if the reasons for these fears are rational or irrational. I will tell you when the time is up."

(*Inform the class when 60 seconds remain. When the time has elapsed, say:*)

"Please spend the next four to five minutes, taking turns, praying out loud for your partner's fears."

3. A Time for Everything . . . (16-A, 16-F)

Time: 15 minutes
Grouping: Groups of five

Leader: *Ask participants to gather in groups of five. When all are in place, say:*

"For the next 15 minutes, each of you please share at least one situation in which a 'cup of cold water' would be more effective *Christian* care than the use of traditional resources. Discuss within your group what form the 'cup of cold water' might take and how other Christian resources might be used later on, or even in conjunction with the cup of cold water. Go ahead."

4. In Your Shoes (16-C)

Time: 7 minutes
Grouping: Whole class

Leader: *Get the class settled down in their chairs and relaxed as much as possible. Read the following slowly:*

"Close your eyes and use your imagination. Imagine yourself driving home from work, school, or shopping. Put yourself in the scene. Go ahead, take a few seconds to imagine it."

(*Pause 10 seconds.*)

"Now imagine your car breaking down. You try to fix it, but no luck. You're on a lonely, deserted stretch of road. It's getting dark, and you're starting to worry. Nobody is coming by. Finally, a car stops. Three people get out and approach you, but something in their manner sets off danger signals in your brain. You panic and start to run, but they grab you and beat you before knocking you to the ground. Two of them kick you while you're lying there. The pain is horrible. You lose consciousness."

(*Pause 10 seconds.*)

"Now, you're conscious again, but you hurt too badly to get up. Slowly, painfully, you crawl to the road so passing cars can see you. A car approaches and slows. The driver is looking at you; his clerical collar indicates that he's a minister or priest. But now he's speeding up. He's not stopping! A few minutes later, another car drives by. Thank God! It's a prominent member of your church who lives down the street from you. She knows you, so you *know* she'll stop. But with scarcely a glance in your direction she speeds on by."

(*Pause 10 seconds.*)

"Your thirst by now is terrible. You no longer have the strength to crawl. A stranger comes by. She stops, approaches you. She doesn't leave! She gives you a drink of water and administers first aid. Taste the water; you've never tasted anything so good. She helps you into her car and takes you to the hospital. Your relief at arriving there changes to fear as the admitting clerk tells you that since you have no money or identification, you cannot be admitted. You are too weak to argue, but the stranger hands the clerk all the money in her purse. She tells the clerk: 'If this isn't enough, I'll be by here in a few days and pay the rest of the bill.' She leaves."

(*Pause 20 seconds. Then slowly read James 2:15-17. Pause 10 more seconds. Then invite them to open their eyes.*)

Note to Leader: Some people are leery of being touched, sometimes with deep-seated reasons. You might want to preface the following exercise with the phrase, "If you are comfortable doing so . . ." and give people a choice about taking part.

5. Cups of Cold Water (16-E, 16-F)

Time: 2 minutes
Grouping: Whole class

Leader: *Ask all to form a circle and then turn to the left. Say:*

"It is time we gave to each other, right now, a little cup of cold water. Spend a minute gently massaging the shoulders of the person in front of you."

Closing

As our last "cup of cold water" in this module, let's spend some time shaking hands with one another. As we do, extend your greeting in words similar to "The peace of the Lord be with you," or "You are sacred," or something from your own heart in your own words.

CHAPTER-MODULE 17

The Evangelism-Caring Connection

Goals

Participants may:

17-A Explore the connection between caring and evangelism.

17-B Discuss what leads to success or failure in evangelism.

17-C Practice the skill and develop the art of sharing God's good news.

17-D Gain increasing sensitivity to daily opportunities for caring evangelism.

17-E Practice fitting the good news to the situations of other group members (making the good news good news *for them*).

17-F Experience the benefits of an evangelistic-caring community in the group.

Opening Prayer

Lord Jesus, when you came to earth to dwell among us, you gave God's love "flesh-and-blood" reality. You never confined the gospel to what you said—it burst forth every time you touched someone with your care. Through the power of the Holy Spirit, you dwell within us. We are your body. Help us make the good news of your love real in the lives of those we encounter each day. Fill us, Lord, with a burning desire not only to proclaim the gospel, but also with a passion to *be* the gospel as we share and care in your name. Amen.

Lead-In

Do you remember "Show and Tell" time when you were in school? Show and Tell remains a favorite activity for children. To be able to tell one's classmates about a special activity is exciting to a child, but to be able to show a memento of the experience adds to his or her delight. Both the showing and the telling enable the classmates to share each other's experiences.

Showing God's love and telling God's love are both important ways to share the gospel—to evangelize. Good evangelism connects the showing and the telling. It doesn't only tell people gospel; it *is* gospel to people.

Our Christian calling to evangelize is closely connected to our calling to care deeply for others. In his book *Life-Style Evangelism*, Joseph Aldrich says: "Remember, people don't care how much (or what) you know until they know how much you care!"[1] We show God's love to others when we love them ourselves. Our concern for the needs of others helps them to believe in God's love. In 1 John 4:12 the writer reminds us: "No one has ever seen God; if we love one another, God lives in us, and his love is perfected in us."

In this module, we will explore the intimate connection between evangelism and caring. We will discover how we can more effectively give God's love "flesh-and-blood" reality.

Discussion Questions

A. What positive feelings do you have about the word *evangelism?* (*Discuss. Then ask:*) What negative ones? (*17-B*)
B. Suppose you were going to share God's love in the following areas.
   • A university campus
   • The poverty-stricken sections of Calcutta, India
   • An affluent suburban community
   • Our own area
   In what ways might your evangelism-caring be the same from place to place? (*Discuss. Then ask:*) In what ways might your evangelism-caring differ? (*17-A, 17-E*)

---

1. Aldrich, Joseph C. *Life-Style Evangelism: Crossing Traditional Boundaries to Reach the Unbelieving World* (Portland, OR: Multnomah Press, 1981), p. 209.

C. There certainly are opportunities for caring evangelism in our neighborhood, your work community, or your circle of acquaintances. How could that caring evangelism be carried out? (17-D)
D. What do you think about this statement: "All that we have been learning, discussing, and doing in our study of *Christian Caregiving—a Way of Life* has been evangelism"? (17-A, 17-D)
E. Have you ever been in a "formal" evangelizing position (evangelism committee, parish visitor, deacon or deaconess, or the like)? In what ways were those situations satisfying? (*Discuss. Then ask:*) In what ways were they dissatisfying? (*Discuss. Then ask:*) How close did those situations come to what the author described as evangelizing? (17-A)
F. How would you evaluate your "informal" evangelizing contacts? (17-D)

Experiential Learning Exercises

1. Evangelism: Bravo! Boo! (17-B, 17-E)

Time: 25-30 minutes
Grouping: Small groups of five, then the class as a whole
Materials: Two sheets of newsprint and one broad-tipped marker for each small group
Advance Preparation: Write the following list on a chalkboard, a transparency, or newsprint, and post it so everyone in the class can see it.

Activities and People Associated with Evangelism:
- Serving on your church's door-to-door calling team
- Billy Graham
- Making a hospital visit
- Televangelists
- A Sunday morning sermon
- Revival meetings
- Serving a meal at a soup kitchen
- Jehovah's Witnesses
- Listening to a grieving widow
- Bumper stickers containing Christian messages
- Mormons

Leader: *Begin by saying:*

"The word *evangelism* stirs varying emotions in each of us. In this activity, we want to identify characteristics of evangelism that elicit positive and negative reactions from us. Please form groups of five."

(*Wait until the groups have formed. Then say:*)

"Each group should select a convener. This person's job will be to keep the group on track and report the group's findings to the whole class. The group should also select a recorder, who will record the group observations."

(*When the groups have appointed the convener/reporter and recorder, distribute two sheets of newsprint and a marker to each recorder. Then say:*)

"Recorders, write the word *Positive* at the top of one of the sheets of newsprint and the word *Negative* at the top of the other. Conveners, read aloud the list of activities and people associated with evangelism and keep your group focused on brainstorming answers to the following questions: 'What is it about the items on the list that gives me positive feelings about evangelism? What is it about the items that makes me feel negative?' The recorder will list the group's answers to each of these questions on the appropriate sheet. You will have 10 minutes of brainstorming time. The object of brainstorming is quantity, not quality. You will have time later to evaluate your listings. Go ahead."

Note to Leader: If your groups need more specific direction, say:

"Let's look at the first item on the list. Ask yourselves: 'How do I feel about this evangelism activity?' Then ask yourselves: 'What is it about this activity that makes me feel positive? Negative?' As you share in your group, the recorder may write words or phrases such as *scary to me* and *feels like we're intruding* as negatives. *Looks like we care* could be listed as a positive."

(*At the end of 10 minutes, signal the groups to stop their brainstorming process. Say:*)

"Your brainstorming time is up. You will now spend five minutes analyzing both of your lists. As you read down your list of positives, do you see any common characteristics repeating themselves? How about your list of negatives? Focusing on those common characteristics, construct two sentences—one summarizing your group's *Positive* list and one summarizing your group's *Negative* list. Any questions?" (*Deal with any questions.*) "You will have five minutes for this task. Go ahead."

(*At the end of five minutes, have the recorders share the groups' findings with the whole class. Discuss any common patterns discovered during the recorders' sharing. This will provide good closure to this activity. You will have 10 minutes for this part of the activity.*)

2. Good News That Works (17-A, 17-F)

Time: 12-15 minutes
Grouping: Pairs
Materials: Each participant will need paper and pen or pencil.

Leader: *Have the class gather into pairs. Once all are in place, say:*

"I would like each of you to think about one or more times when good news was communicated effectively to you. If a specific act of caring was involved in that evangelism, think of how it tied into the experience. Take a minute alone to think individually of such a time and perhaps jot some notes if you like. I'll let you know when a minute is up."

(*After a minute has elapsed, say:*) "Go ahead and share your thoughts with your partner. Take about five minutes each."

(*Inform them when half the time has elapsed so they can switch roles. Close the exercise at the end of 10 minutes or so.*)

3. The Whole Truth and Nothing but the Truth (17-C, 17-F)

Time: 25-30 minutes
Grouping: Individual, then groups of three
Materials: All will need paper, pen or pencil, and writing space.

Leader: *After all have a place to work and are equipped with pen and paper, read the following:*

"Evangelism happens in what we do and say. In this exercise we are going to concentrate on what we say. A witness is one who tells what he or she has experienced. Spend 10 minutes writing down your account of the good news you have experienced in Jesus. Make it personal, concentrating on Jesus' impact upon you. After you finish, you will share some or all of what you have written with a small group. You may begin."

(After 10 minutes, say:)

"Now gather in groups of three."

(When the groups have been formed, say:)

"Imagine that each of you has been called to testify in a court of law regarding the nature of your relationship with Jesus Christ. Each of you in turn will share your written witness with your small group. You will have about 15 minutes for this activity."

(At five-minute intervals, inform the group that it is time to call the next witness. After about 15 minutes, conclude the exercise.)

4. Daily News for Daily Needs (17-D, 17-E, 17-F)

Time: 25 minutes
Grouping: Groups of three

Leader: *Have the class gather in groups of three. Then read the following:*

"Al just lost his job. It is one month before Christmas, and he is worried that the loss of his job will ruin Christmas for his wife and their four children. In your group, discuss ways in which you could say, do, and be the gospel to Al. You will have about three minutes. Begin."

(After three minutes, read the following:)

"Your sixteen-year-old niece is visiting you. She appears quite depressed. You know that she has recently broken up with her boyfriend. How could you say, do, and be the gospel to your niece? You will have about three minutes to discuss this in your group. Go ahead."

(After three minutes, read the following:)

"Each of you share with your partners a description of a person you know who needs God's good news. Do not share names or information that might reveal the person's identity. Together discuss how you might share the good news with that person through how you live, how you care, and what you say. Take 15 minutes for this."

(At five-minute intervals, inform the groups that it is time for the next person to share. Close the activity after 15 minutes or so.)

Closing

Advance Preparation: Write the words in the box below on a chalkboard, transparency, or a sheet of newsprint. Writing the first letter of each of the words in a different color will give the word *GOSPEL* more emphasis. Draw attention to this visual aid as you begin this benediction.

Go	to your world; be the Body of Christ.
Offer	peace, hope, and love; he paid the price.
Show	his compassion to each hurting heart.
Proclaim	his salvation; his blessings impart.
Evangelize	and care—Both vital to do.
Live	so God's love is completed in you.

CHAPTER-MODULE 18

Celebrating Results

Goals

Participants may:

18-A Understand the distinction between process-oriented and result-oriented caring.

18-B Discuss the benefits of being process-oriented in Christian life and ministry.

18-C Display awareness that God is process-oriented.

18-D Experience the results of distinctively Christian caring with the group.

Note to Leader: Because the format of the final session can take more than one direction and might include preplanning by group members, read Chapter-Module 20 *before* your next-to-last class. There are several possibilities that you would need to take up with the participants now. If you want to have a celebration or a worship service, you will need to plan it now.

Opening Prayer

Make me an instrument of your healing, Lord.
> I offer my small part to the caring harmony of your people, and
> I play each note trusting in your direction.
I will celebrate those moments, Lord,
> When the symphony of your love
> Brings healing to one of your hurting children. Amen.

Lead-In

Danny received his first bicycle for his sixth birthday. He was anxious to learn to ride it so he could ride with the other children in the neighborhood. Danny's father, Ed, was anxious to teach his son to ride the bicycle. That night at the dinner table, Ed told Danny all about the skills he would need to know in order to ride his bicycle. After dinner Danny still did not know how to ride his bike. Later that evening in the garage, Ed gave his son a quick course on the mechanical functioning of his new bicycle. Still, Danny did not know how to ride his bicycle. The next day Ed bought Danny a video about bicycle safety. After watching the video, Danny remained unable to ride his bicycle.

All that Ed is doing for Danny will eventually enhance his appreciation of bicycling, but the only way for Danny to learn to ride his bike is to experience the process of riding a bike. *He* must steer. *He* must balance. *He* must fall down a few times. Yes, Ed can provide a steadying hand, share some encouraging words, and support Danny in his attempts. But learning to ride a bike is a process, and Danny must go through the process. Only then will his goal of riding a bicycle be realized.

One of the great temptations in caring for another is wanting to jump right in, rearrange a person's life, and immediately fix whatever problems that person might have. The alternative—entering into another's pain, suffering with and supporting that person while he or she works through a crisis—is much more difficult. It is also the only way to help effectively.

In our study of *Christian Caregiving—a Way of Life* we have been learning much about the process of caring for others. We have learned that the results of our caring are in God's hands. In this module, we will concentrate on understanding the difference between being result-centered and being process-centered; we will also identify and celebrate the results that God freely gives.

Discussion Questions

A. Our lives as Christians might be described as a continuing process of growing in God. How can understanding this help us to be more process-oriented in our Christian caring? (*18-B, 18-C*)

B. Let's say you have a friend who is going through a painful divorce. How might you "push for results"? (*Discuss. Then ask:*) How might you focus on process? (*18-A, 18-B*)

C. What do you think of the statement on page 138 that "results start happening when you stop pushing for them"? (*18-C*)

D. Look at the three passages near the top of page 142 of *Christian Caregiving—a Way of Life*. What do those passages have to do with "the process of Christian living"? (*Discuss. Then ask:*) Look up Philippians 2:13. What light does that shed? (*18-B*)

E. Look at the last paragraph on page 146 in *Christian Caregiving—a Way of Life*. Which of these reminders/cautions particularly strike you? Why? (*18-C*)

F. What role does suffering play in the Christian process? (*18-C*)

G. If Jesus commanded us to actively do the following: "Make disciples of all nations" and "Save the lost," how can we focus on the process rather than on the goals? (*Discuss. Then ask:*) How might the author respond to this, and what can you add to the author's response? (*18-B, 18-C*)

Experiential Learning Exercises

1. Don't Bother Me with Facts—I Want Results! (18-B, 18-D)

Time: 10-12 minutes
Grouping: Pairs

Leader: *Ask the class to gather in pairs. Then read the following:*

"In the next 10 minutes, each of you in turn describe to your partner a time in your own life or in that of someone you know when results started happening only when you or someone else stopped pushing for them. I'll let you know when half the time has elapsed. Begin."

(*When five minutes have elapsed, remind them to move to the other person.*)

2. Results vs. Process (18-A, 18-B)

Time: 20 minutes
Grouping: Groups of five
Materials: Each small group will need paper and a pen or pencil.

Leader: *Ask the class to assemble into groups of five. Wait until this has occurred. Then say:*
"Now choose a convener."
(*Pause briefly. Then say:*)
"This exercise has four steps. The first step is for your group to choose an example of a personal or life crisis, either actual or invented. That crisis will be the focus for the exercise. You will have two minutes to select a crisis. Go ahead."
(*Answer any questions and work with any group that might need assistance. Examples of crises that they might choose are: death of a spouse, being in the hospital, loss of a job, or the birth of triplets. After all the groups have selected a crisis, say:*)
"As a group, focus on this crisis and think of as many results goals for your caregiving as you can. Conveners, please write down all the ideas. Take five minutes for this. Go ahead."
(*At the end of five minutes, say:*)
"In the next five minutes, brainstorm and record as many process goals as you can for caring for someone going through this crisis. Go ahead."
(*At the end of five minutes, say:*)
"Finally, spend five minutes discussing how your caring would be different if you focused on result goals rather than process goals."
(*Close this exercise after five minutes.*)

3. Caring for Betty and Beverly (18-B, 18-D)

Time: 25-30 minutes
Grouping: Groups of five, then the class as a whole

Leader: *Divide the class into groups of five. After all are in place, ask each group to choose a convener. Then read the following:*
"I'll read you two hypothetical situations in which someone is in need of Christian care. After I'm done with each one, you'll have

some time to talk about it. Ready? The first situation involves Betty, a young woman going through a difficult divorce. She has stopped attending church, perhaps because she believes she is unworthy to associate with 'good' people. She is isolated; she spends most of each day in her house with her two preschool children. She has a great deal of resentment toward her husband coupled with a great deal of guilt about her own conduct. She seems to have lost faith, not only in men, but in people in general, maybe even in God. Her life seems to have no focus or purpose. Discuss in your groups what you might do to provide Christian care to Betty and how you might go about it. You have five minutes. Go ahead."

(Allow them to talk for five minutes. Inform them when 30 seconds remain. Then say:)

"Next, take a look on pages 143-146 of *Christian Caregiving—a Way of Life*, where there is a list of 11 distinctive results that God might provide through your care. Look at these and decide, as a group, which you might reasonably expect as the results of Christian care. For example, take the first goal—community. Can you see the possibility that God might allow Betty to develop stronger ties to the Christian community as a result of your care? Go through the 11 results and apply them to Betty. Again, you have five minutes. Go ahead."

(Inform them when 30 seconds remain. After five minutes, say:)

"Let's take another situation. This time the person for whom you are caring is Beverly, a 90-year-old widow in a nursing home. She has no family or friends left. Her physical condition is poor; she has very little time left. She is unresponsive and incoherent; neither you nor the medical staff can tell for sure whether or not she is aware of the fact she has a visitor. Which of the 11 results can you reasonably expect for Beverly? Take five minutes and decide as a group. Go ahead."

(Allow them to talk for five minutes. Inform them when 30 seconds remain. Then ask:)

"Were any of the groups optimistic about obtaining fantastic results with Beverly? (*Pause for responses.*) The questions I want you to discuss in your groups are: In situations like Beverly's in which God is not likely to grant us much in the way of tangible results, what should we be trying to do? What does God want from us in situations like these? Go ahead, take three or four minutes and talk about it."

(Inform them when 30 seconds remain. After four minutes, open the discussion to the whole class for a few minutes.)

4. In God's Hands (18-C, 18-D)

Time: 7-8 minutes
Grouping: Whole group

Note to Leader: In this activity, it is important that you give the class a chance to relax before beginning. Read slowly in a soothing voice. If you use this activity, you may wish to use it as the final activity, moving immediately into the closing.

Leader: *Begin the exercise by saying:*
"As we begin this exercise, it is important for you to relax. Assume a comfortable position in your chair. Close your eyes. Breathe deeply and slowly. Relax."
(Pause 10 seconds. Then say:)
"Think of someone in your life who needs care. In your mind, see that person's face; feel his or her need."
(Pause 10 seconds. Then say:)
"Imagine this. God is walking toward you, carrying a large canvas sack. He places the sack at your feet and says to you: 'In this sack are my care goals for your friend in need. I, too, have seen your friend's face. I, too, have felt your friend's need. I want you to help me take this sack to our friend.' Consider how you feel about God's request."
(Pause 10 seconds. Then say:)
"You look at the canvas sack and know that it contains the care that your friend needs. You impulsively bend over to pick up the sack. Suddenly, you realize that the sack is too heavy for you to lift. You cry out to God: 'Help me! I cannot carry this sack!'
"Gently, God responds: 'Look in the sack. Inside you will find a heavy, gift-wrapped package. That gift is my result goal for your friend. It belongs to me. Place it in my hands. I will carry it. What remains in the sack are the makings for a party—streamers, horns, hats, decorations, cups, and plates. They are the process goals. You can carry those. You will precede me on the path to our friend,

carrying these on my behalf. You will set the scene. I will come behind you, bringing the gift, the result.'

"You look into God's eyes. They are filled with love for you and for your friend. Think about how you feel now."

(*Pause 10 seconds. Then say:*)

"Now return to the 'here and now.' Take a deep breath and open your eyes when you're ready."

(*Pause to allow participants to re-orient themselves.*)

Closing

May God's mighty hand
    steady our steps,
    strengthen our spirits, and
    sustain our hope
As we engage in the process of Christian caregiving.
May we raise our hands to God
    in thankfulness,
    in praise, and
    in celebration,
Remembering always in whose hand all success rests.
Amen.

CHAPTER-MODULE 19

Hope-Full Caregiving

Goals

Participants may:

19-A Gain understanding of Christian hope.

19-B Experience the blessings of Christian hope with the group.

19-C See how God uses the hope residing in a Christian to kindle hope in others.

19-D Grasp the many practical implications of the "now/not yet" hope of Christians.

19-E Empathize with other group members' disappointments and despair.

19-F Experience Christian community.

Opening Prayer

Lord Jesus, we stand at your tomb in amazement. It is empty. You are alive!

Like the women at your grave, we too want to run and share with everyone the good news that you have conquered death.

Hope has replaced our fear. Our minds know this even when our hearts do not. You will always be with us to help us through every trial in our lives.

Your hope is so wonderful. We praise you for your compassion and care.

Teach us to live in your hope and to cast out despair, so others may know your love. Amen.

Lead-In

When the hurts of life appear, some often flail their arms in vigorous attempts to resist the emotional undertow. But the harder they try to escape the rising tide of their problems, the more the swirling whirlpool of discouragement, depression, and defeat seem destined to pull them under.

Just when all seems lost, someone throws out a lifeline. God offers hope.

Hope buoys us up, keeping us secure during the rough times. It rescues us from despair.

Hope is not something we can generate within ourselves. It is not a quality we will find if only we try harder. Hope is a gift of God.

So, how does God produce this precious gift? It is through the very crisis itself that God develops within us this vital, life-affirming quality.

The Apostle Paul speaks of this relationship between crisis and hope in his letter to the Romans. He writes:

> And not only that, but we also boast in our sufferings, knowing that suffering produces endurance, and endurance produces character, and character produces hope, and hope does not disappoint us, because God's love has been poured into our hearts through the Holy Spirit that has been given to us" (Romans 5:3-5).

Yes, God uses the very trials of our lives to produce the hope that helps us, not merely to survive, but to prosper and thrive as well. And to bestow that gift, he often uses the willing hands and feet of those who serve him—you and me.

Thus, hope is a special Christian resource, one to use frequently in your caring and relating. It's a birthright and a blessing we can pass on to others that will strengthen and encourage them.

Hope can be a powerful force in people's lives, especially in this age, an age characterized as "hopeless" and "full of despair." The hope we Christians offer shines forth as the genuine object in a world filled with cheap imitations.

So, let's be bold. Let's lift high the gift of hope to our world, and let it shine into all the darkened corners of despair.

Let's use our time of study to rejoice in this distinctive gift and seek ways to effectively instill hope in the lives of those for whom we care.

Discussion Questions

A. Can you think of a time when you had no hope or had almost lost all hope? Describe the feeling. (*19-A, 19-E*)

B. The author lists nine ways on pages 148-153 that we can be instruments of hope for others:

Sticking with them	Emphasizing the positive
Being available	Realizing failures and
Reducing anxiety	limitations
Sharing the stories of others	Jesus with you
Accepting the other	Being distinctively Christian

What are some situations where Jesus acted as an instrument of hope in any of these nine ways? (*19-A, 19-C*)

C. What does it mean that Christian hope is both now and not yet? (*19-D*)

D. How can you continue to hope when your hope never seems to come true or seems too far away? (*19-C, 19-E*)

E. In what types of situations would it be appropriate to share spoken words of hope? (*Discuss. Then ask:*) What about inappropriate situations? (*19-A*)

F. How does your ultimate hope in Jesus Christ help you in your caring relationships? (*19-B, 19-C*)

Experiential Learning Exercises

1. A Hopeful Search (19-A, 19-F)

Time: 15-20 minutes

Grouping: Four roughly equal-sized groups (If the class is small, you might choose to operate with two or three groups total.)

Materials: All need a Bible, pen or pencil, and paper

Leader: *After dividing the class into four groups or less, designate each group with a letter: A, B, C, etc. Then say:*
"Now choose a convener for your group."
(Pause briefly. Then continue:)
"We are going to search the Bible to find passages that deal with the distinctively Christian concept of hope. Each group will consider a different aspect of hope.

"I'll assign your topic and then I want your group to find one or more passages to illustrate it. We will do two rounds of searches and you will have five minutes to carry out each search.

"Quality is more important than quantity. But if you've found a passage that you like and I haven't called time yet, try to find more. Any questions?"
(Deal with any questions. Then continue:)
"All right, Group *A*, look for passages offering assurance that God will stick with us no matter what. Go ahead, take five minutes and come up with as much scriptural assurance as possible. "Group *B*, find passages that assure us that God is always available to us any time we call on him. Go ahead.

"Group *C*, find passages showing men or women of God working their way through troubles far greater than those we are likely to face. Go ahead.

"Group *D*, find passages that convince us that God accepts us, just as we are. Go ahead."
(Inform the class when 30 seconds remain. When five minutes are up, have the convener of each group share with the whole class one or more of the passages they discovered. Then say:)
"Group *A*, find passages in which Jesus emphasized the positive aspects of people. Go ahead.

"Group *B*, find passages showing us that human failures, weaknesses, and frailties are important to God and are used by him for his own purpose. Go ahead.

"Group *C*, find one or more passages assuring us of Jesus' presence with us. Go ahead.

"Group *D*, please find passages speaking directly of Christian hope. Go ahead and begin."
(Inform the class when 30 seconds remain. When five minutes are up, have each group share one or more passages they discovered.)

2. Personal Experience of Hope (19-B, 19-F)

Time: 10-15 minutes
Grouping: Small groups of five

Leader: *Have the class divide into groups of five. After the groups have assembled, say:*
"Now choose a convener."
(Pause briefly. Then continue:)
"I'd like several members in each group to share an experience you had in which hope played an important part. Tell about a time in your life in which distinctively Christian hope made it possible to continue despite difficult circumstances. Think about this for a few moments, then share with the others. If someone cannot immediately think of an experience, just say 'pass' and go on to the next person."

3. Sharing Hope (19-B, 19-F)

Time: 15 minutes
Grouping: Groups of three

Leader: *Ask the class to assemble in groups of three and sit facing each other. When all are in place, say:*
"I'd like you to think of a situation that initially appeared to be quite hopeless. It can be something that happened either to you or to another person.
"Have the first member of your group share the incident. Then discuss in your group ways to share hope with a person in that circumstance.
"Then go on to the next person until all have had an opportunity to share. You will have 15 minutes to complete this activity."
(Give five-minute interval warnings, and conclude the exercise after 15 minutes.)

4. A Picture of Hope (19-D, 19-F)

Time: 20-25 minutes
Grouping: Individual, then class as a whole
Materials: A supply of felt-tip pens, pencils, crayons, modeling clay, and the like
Advance Preparation: Prepare some work areas with newspapers spread on tables for some of the messier forms of creativity.

Leader: *Read the following:*

"St. Paul writes in Romans 8:22 that all creation groans in labor, eagerly awaiting the revealing of God's children at Christ's second coming. The creation, too, participates in Christian hope. This is Paul's creative 'picture of hope.' Each of you creatively try to picture God's hope in some way. You might wish to write a poem or a short story, draw a picture, or sculpt something. Depending on what medium of creativity you choose, you can work at these tables or in a quiet corner. Come up and choose the materials you would like to work with. Good creating! You have 10 minutes."

(After they are finished, depending on the size of the class, you can have each person briefly share with the class what they made and the symbolism behind it, or divide them into small groups to do so.)

5. Impossible Hope (19-A, 19-D)

Time: 15-20 minutes
Grouping: Individual, then pairs
Materials: Pen or pencil, paper
Advance Preparation: List the following three statements on a chalkboard, overhead, or newsprint for use during the writing of the fax:

    1. Share with God how you felt about your impossible circumstance at that time.

    2. Reflect upon what actually happened.

    3. Describe how you feel about the situation now.

    Also write the following four questions on the chalkboard, overhead, or newsprint, and keep them covered until the discussion time:

    1. What was your impossible situation?

    2. What was the outcome?

    3. What made the difference?

    4. How can we encourage a care receiver who thinks his or her situation is hopeless or impossible?

Leader: *Distribute paper and a pencil or pen to those who need them. Then say:*

"Do you find fax machines as convenient as I do? I've often thought it would be helpful during times of confusion to be able to fax an immediate description of my problem to God. We are going to do that in this exercise.

"Think of a time in your Christian life when you felt God was calling you to do the impossible. Write a fax to God about that experience. Share with God how you felt about the circumstance at that time, reflect upon what actually happened, and describe how you feel about the situation now."

(Allow about 8-10 minutes for participants to write their faxes to God. Then say:)

"Find a partner and sit together."

(While this is happening, reveal the second set of questions you prepared in advance. Then say:)

"Think again about your impossible situation. Discuss with your partner your answers to these four questions. You'll have about five minutes each. Go ahead."

7. Heroic Christians (19-C, 19-E)

Time: 20-25 minutes
Grouping: Groups of three, then class as a whole
Materials: Pencil or pen, paper

Leader: *Divide the class into groups of three. Wait until this has happened. Then say:*

"In this exercise we are going to role-play an encounter between a person facing a difficult situation and a friend who comes to visit.

"In your groups, quickly decide who is person *A*, person *B*, and person *C*."

(Pause briefly. Then say:)

"Here are the parts you will take in the role play. *A*, you will play the role of the person in crisis. *B*, you are the friend who comes to visit. *C*, you are the observer who is to watch and take notes during the role play.

"In just a moment, I am going to have the *B*'s come forward for some special instructions. While I am talking to the *B*'s, I want the *A*'s and *C*'s to develop a brief biography for person *A*. Decide what difficult situation *A* is facing, what attitude *A* has toward it, and what kind of troubled emotions *A* is generally feeling.

(Meet with the B's in a location beyond the hearing range of the class and share the following privileged information.)

[Privileged Information for B's Only]

In this role play, I want you to be friendly but insensitive to the struggles of person *A*. Whenever *A* begins to share about his or her situation, I want you to tell person *A* about another Christian who has encountered a similar set of circumstances. Talk at great length about how that person's problems were much more severe than person *A*'s difficulties. Keep pushing to minimize the seriousness of person *A*'s problems as you talk about this other individual. Make person *A*'s difficulties seem minor.

Describe the courageous way this other Christian rose above his or her circumstances, without ever expressing any negative emotions, or losing faith and hope in God. Portray this other individual as a model of Christian virtue, stamina, and fortitude in the face of adversity. Make person *A* feel very diminished in comparison to this heroic Christian. Do you have any questions? (*Answer any questions about the role play.*) Go back to your groups and wait, and I'll give further instructions to all of you before we begin."

(*After the B's have returned to their seats, say:*)

"Now we are going to role-play a visit between *A* and *B*. Please stand to greet one another at the door and then be seated for the visit. C's, remember to take notes on what you observe. I'll give you about three minutes for the role play. Go ahead and begin."

(*After about three minutes, get the participants' attention and discuss the following questions, spending three or four minutes on each.*)

1. How did those of you in crisis feel?
2. How did the visitors feel?
3. What did the observers notice?
4. How should the stories of others be shared in order to instill hope?

Closing

May the hope that flows from Jesus' life, death, and resurrection fill you fully, giving you faith for your despair, joy for your sorrow, peace during your times of stress. May you grow in compassion and love for all and share the good news with those you encounter. Amen.

CHAPTER-MODULE 20

The Thrill of It All

Goals

Participants may:

20-A Reflect upon the experience of studying *Christian Caregiving—a Way of Life* together.

20-B Rejoice in what they have learned and experienced.

20-C Come together for a "closing" to the class.

20-D Plan together for future use of what they have learned and experienced.

20-E Review together the high points of the study.

20-F Summarize for one another the most vital insights gained in class.

20-G Experience Christian community.

Note to Leader: If you are following the suggested two modules per session, you may wish to have a time of fellowship in place of this final module. Each participant could bring some snacks to share. You could use the "Opening Prayer" and parts of the "Lead-In" to begin the time of fellowship and end by singing a well-known song (the common doxology, for example) and the "Closing." Or, this final segment could combine fellowship and a worship service. Other possibilities include extending the midpoint break or the closing time, beginning the final session with a potluck meal, or scheduling a concluding half-day retreat.

Opening Prayer

Heavenly Father, to everything there is a season and a time for every purpose under heaven. A time to learn, a time to grow, a time to become a bit more the person you created us to be.

Thank you, God, for changing us, for building us, for making us better equipped through this class to care for others.

We celebrate what you have done for us—your great love in the sacrifice of your son Jesus—and offer this love to others in his name. Amen.

Lead-In

Here we are at the end of our journey together, and what a trip it's been!

We've probably made new friends, deepened existing relationships, gained fresh understandings and skills, and developed a whole new set of attitudes about caring.

Yes, our trip is almost over. Soon we will return to our everyday lives. We will resume our usual routines and pick up where we left off, before our journey began.

But, stop. Wait a minute. Listen!

Can you hear it over the din of the milling crowds?

A whistle is quietly echoing in the far-off distance. A gentle clackity-clack, more like a feeble vibration than a sound, is becoming more apparent.

Another train is coming into the station. This is not the end of our journey at all, but merely a station stop to change directions.

We have learned much from the journey so far. For one thing, we will travel lighter now, leaving behind the excess baggage of old habits, attitudes, and self-doubts that hindered us on our caregiving journey before.

On this next leg of our trip, we will carry with us some basic essentials of the Christian caregiver: prayer, forgiveness, absolution, the Word of God, hope, blessings, and the living water from whom we will draw "cups of cold water" to offer to our fellow passengers along the way.

Where will this journey lead us?

We can't even begin to guess what adventures lie ahead of us on this quest. We simply know that this is a journey into caring and service, and it is ours to pursue for a lifetime.

In this final module we will look back on our journey. We will remember the highlights of our class, the special blessings we have received, the growth we have experienced. We will also look forward, anticipating how God will use our skills, our compassion, and our love in the future.

So, today is a time of farewell as we say "good-bye" to our class. But it is also a time of expectations as we say "hello" to a future filled with hope.

It's time to step up on the platform. Christ, our conductor, is calling, "All aboard."

Discussion Questions

A. How ready do you feel to go out and exercise uniquely Christian caregiving and relating? (*20-A, 20-D*)
B. How might your caring be different since you've read and studied this book? (*20-A, 20-F*)
C. What are some of the insights you have gained in studying *Christian Caregiving—a Way of Life*? (*20-A, 20-F*)
D. What unique gifts do we as Christian caring persons bring to our hurt and broken world? (*20-E*)
E. How can we apply what we have learned to make our congregation an even more distinctively Christian group of people? (*20-D*)
F. How do you intend to share with others the gifts you received in this study? (*Discuss. Then ask:*) Who are some people with whom you would like to share what you have received? (*20-F*)

Experiential Learning Exercises

1. Dear God (20-B, 20-G)

Time: 20 minutes
Grouping: Individually, then in pairs
Materials: Each participant will need pen or pencil and paper for this exercise.

Leader: *Read the following:*

"As a way of remembering and completing our experience of studying *Christian Caregiving—a Way of Life,* each of you go off by yourself for 10 minutes and write a letter to God. You might want to have your letter contain any or all of these four things:

1. Thanking God for the experience.
2. Planning with God how you are going to use the skills and insights you gained.
3. Asking God the questions about caring that are still unanswered for you.
4. Asking God to continue empowering you for your service to him.

"Be prepared to share this letter with another person. I'll tell you when 10 minutes are up."

(At the end of 10 minutes, have the class divide into pairs and ask them to share their letters. Tell them they have five to ten minutes for this.)

2. Learning, and Using What You Learned (20-A, 20-C, 20-E)

Time: 20-40 minutes

Grouping: Groups of five

Advance Preparation: Write the following questions on a chalkboard or newsprint:

1. In *one* sentence, what have you learned from this class?
2. What distinctive gifts have each of you discovered in yourself during this study? What gifts can you name in others in our group?
3. What was the best moment for you during this study?
4. What have you learned about yourself as a Christian and about your relationship with God during these weeks?
5. How have you already used what you learned in these sessions?

Divide the class into groups of five. Ask the small groups to discuss the questions for 20-40 minutes. You may want to include a time for the whole class to discuss in the large group. If so, shorten the small group discussion time accordingly.

3. Goodhearted Graffiti (20-A, 20-B, 20-F)

Time: 10-15 minutes

Grouping: Class as a whole

Materials: 15- to 20-foot piece of butcher paper, a supply of felt-tip pens
Advance Preparation: Tape the blank sheet of butcher paper to a nearby wall, portable room divider, or large bulletin board. Move any obstructing furniture or objects to allow easy access.

Leader: *Begin by saying:*

"We have made many discoveries during our experience of studying *Christian Caregiving—a Way of Life*. Now, it's time to rejoice in what we have learned and experienced.

"In just a moment, we are going to use felt-tip markers to write some goodhearted graffiti about our time together these past weeks. Write about your memorable class experiences, the ideas or skills you learned, words of appreciation and affirmation to other class participants, and insights that you have gained from this course.

"Feel free to include symbols and designs as part of your farewell comments."

(*Point out the location of the butcher paper banner and the felt-tip pens. Then say:*)

"By the way, be careful to keep your writing confined to the butcher paper, so we don't have to do any explaining to the church custodian tomorrow."

(*Be sure to allow time for the participants to read the comments of the other class members before you conclude the exercise.*)

Closing

May our God who brought us together for this season now go with us on our journey. May he continually bring to our remembrance the love, the fellowship, the care, and the growth we have shared together. May he fill our hearts with courage and joy so that we can go from this place willing and able to share our gift of distinctively Christian care to those we encounter. And may the continual presence of God the Father, the Son, and the Holy Spirit be with us now, and always. Amen.

APPENDIX A

Getting the Word Out: Publicity Helps

Sample Bulletin Inserts

The basic format of inserts for your bulletin is: lead-in, schedule, course information, and conclusion.

Provided are three different lead-ins for you to choose from, and two "schedule" paragraphs, depending upon whether or not you intend to include a retreat in the course. In the examples that follow, variable information is enclosed within brackets [like this]. The first version is complete, and the other two are alternate lead-ins for you to use.

Sample Bulletin Insert 1

Distinctively Christian

Do I, as a Christian, have anything unique to offer my friends and family when they are hurting? What makes the care that Christians offer different from that offered by everyone else? How can I live and care for others in a way that is distinctively Christian?

Have you ever asked these questions? Kenneth Haugk did, and in the course of answering them he wrote a book entitled *Christian Caregiving—a Way of Life*. Dr. Haugk is the founder and Executive Director of the Stephen Series system of lay caring ministry. [*Name of your congregation*] is offering a [*7-week—10-week*] course to study this book and explore ways that we can live and care in a more distinctively Christian manner.

159

Beginning on [*day of week, month, date*], the class will meet every [*day of week*] from [*time*] to [*time*] for seven weeks at [*place*]. We have also scheduled a Friday evening and an all-day Saturday retreat for [*dates*].

or

Beginning on [*day of week, month, date*], the class will meet every [*day of week*] from [*time*] to [*time*] for 10 weeks at [*place where first meeting will be*].

The course will be led by [*name of leader(s)*]. The cost is [*$ amount*], which will include a copy of the book for each participant, plus supplies and refreshments. The registration deadline is [*date*].

Call or talk to [*name of contact and phone number*] to sign up or obtain more information.

Sample Bulletin Insert 2

Live It!

"I believe it, but how do I live it?" Christianity is more than a set of beliefs; it is a way of life. If our beliefs do not affect our living, what good are they? So, how do we live what we believe?

[*Name of congregation*] is offering a new course that will address that question and help you find some answers, using the book *Christian Caregiving—a Way of Life* by Kenneth Haugk as our study tool. Dr. Haugk, a pastor and clinical psychologist, is the founder of the Stephen Series system of lay caring ministry.

[*Repeat one of the "schedule" paragraphs plus the concluding two paragraphs from Sample Bulletin Insert 1.*]

Sample Bulletin Insert 3

Have You Ever . . . ?

Have you ever had a friend or neighbor who was hurting spiritually or emotionally? Have you ever wanted to share with another person the love and care that you may have received from fellow Christians? Have you ever known someone who was being consumed by guilt and needed the freedom that God's forgiveness brings?

Have we got a course for you! [*Name of your congregation*] is going to offer a [*7-week/10-week*] course on the book *Christian Caregiving—a Way of Life*, by Dr. Kenneth Haugk, a pastor and clinical psychologist who is the founder of the Stephen Series system of lay caring ministry. The course will help you discover ways to become a distinctively Christian caregiver.

[*Repeat one of the "schedule" paragraphs plus the two concluding paragraphs from Sample Bulletin Insert 1.*]

Sample Letters

Here are some sample letters for use in special mailings or for inclusion in the congregation's newsletter.

Sample 1: The First Time the Course Is Offered

Dear Members of [*name of congregation*]:

We will soon be offering a new class that will enable us to better understand who we are as Christians and how we can live our lives in a distinctively Christian way. This class will be relevant for anyone who has ever wondered: What makes an act of caring Christian? What can be pointed to in caring or relating that could be called "Christian?" Who am I as a Christian?

This course is based on the book *Christian Caregiving—a Way of Life* by Kenneth Haugk. Dr. Haugk is the founder of the Stephen Series system of lay caring ministry and is an ordained minister and clinical psychologist.

Beginning on [*day of week, month, date*], the class will meet every [*day of week*] from [*time*] to [*time*] for seven weeks at [*place*]. We have also scheduled a Friday evening and an all-day Saturday retreat for [*dates*].

or

Beginning on [*day of week, month, date*], the class will meet every [*day of week*] from [*time*] to [*time*] for 10 weeks at [*place where first meeting will be*].

The class will be taught by [*name of leader(s)*]. Each session will be a combination of lecture, discussion, and practice of caring skills. The 20 topics to be covered will include such areas as:

- God, You, and Me
- Why Care?
- Touching Spiritual Depths
- Servanthood vs. Servitude
- The Bible
- A Cup of Cold Water
- Celebrating Results
- The Thrill of It All

There will be a registration fee of [*$ amount*], which covers the cost of the text, other supplies, and refreshments. Your registration indicates your commitment to attend all sessions.

The course offers a rich mixture of practical theology, psychology, and sociology that will help you live your Christianity fully— as a practicing, caring Christian. If you are interested in attending, please fill out the form below and return it to [*place or person*]. [*Typical Closing*], [*Name*]

....

☐ YES, I am interested in taking part in the course "Christian Caregiving—a Way of Life." Enclosed is $_____.

Name: _____

Address: _____

_____

Phone: _____

Signature: _____

☐ I am interested in taking this course, but cannot do so now. Please let me know the next time the class is offered.

Sample 2: For Subsequent Offerings of the Course

Dear Members of [*name of congregation*]:

We will again be offering the course entitled "Christian Caregiving—a Way of Life" using the book by the same title as our primary resource. We are pleased to be able to offer this course again, based on the extremely positive reactions to it.

Thus far, [*number*] individuals from our congregation have completed the course. Here are some of their reactions:

[*Insert at least two quotes from participants.*]

The author of *Christian Caregiving—a Way of Life* is Kenneth Haugk, who is also the founder of the Stephen Series system of lay caring ministry. Dr. Haugk is an ordained minister and a clinical psychologist. His book centers on the crucial question: "What is distinctive about Christian caring and relating?"

The course is practical. Always the emphasis is on *What does this mean for me?* and *How do I put it into practice in my life?* The teaching methods combine lecture, discussion, and practical application exercises, with the accent on the latter. [*Name of leader(s)*] will conduct the course. The 20 topics you will explore include:

- God as the Curegiver
- Move Over, Freud!
- Ministering to the Whole Person
- A Surprise Gift: Forgiveness
- Tools of Your Trade: Their Use and Abuse
- Prayer
- The Evangelism-Caring Connection
- Hope-Full Caregiving

Beginning on [*day of week, month, date*], the class will meet every [*day of week*] from [*time*] to [*time*] for seven weeks at [*place*]. We have also scheduled a Friday evening and an all-day Saturday retreat for [*dates*].

or

Beginning on [*day of week, month, date*], the class will meet every [*day of week*] from [*time*] to [*time*] for 10 weeks at [*place where first meeting will be*].

There will be a registration fee of [*$ amount*], which covers the cost of the text, other supplies, and refreshments. Your registration indicates your commitment to attend all sessions.

What a blessing this course has been to those who have taken part in it! We invite and encourage you to complete the form below and return it to [*place or person*].

[*Typical Closing*],
[*Name*]

....

☐ YES, I am interested in taking part in the course "Christian Caregiving—a Way of Life." Enclosed is $_____.

Name: _____

Address: _____

_____

Phone: _____

Signature: _____

☐ I am interested in taking this course, but cannot do so now. Please let me know the next time the class is offered.

Sample 3: Letter to Special Groups in the Congregation

To: The Members of [name of organization]
     % [name of chairperson]

Dear Christian Friends,

We will soon be offering a special course based on the book *Christian Caregiving—a Way of Life* by Kenneth Haugk. The book deals theologically, psychologically, and—most of all—very practically with questions such as:

- Why should we care for others?
- How can our living and caregiving be distinctively Christian?
- How can we use the Bible and prayer in our Christian caring and relating?

[Optional: You may want to insert questions that are targeted more specifically at the group you are addressing.]

Since your group is an important part of [name of congregation], we are eager for you to know about this opportunity to increase your effectiveness as Christian caring persons. Christian caregiving is an important part of anyone's life, and of ministry in and around our congregation and our community. Your attendance at this course could prove an enormous blessing not only to you personally but also to [name of the group].

Beginning on [*day of week, month, date*], the class will meet every [*day of week*] from [*time*] to [*time*] for seven weeks at [*place*]. We have also scheduled a Friday evening and an all-day Saturday retreat for [*dates*].

or

Beginning on [*day of week, month, date*], the class will meet every [*day of week*] from [*time*] to [*time*] for 10 weeks at [*place where first meeting will be*].

The class will be taught by [*name of leader(s)*]. Each session will be a combination of lecture, discussion, and practice of caring skills. The 20 topics to be covered will include such areas as:

- God, You, and Me
- Why Care?
- Touching Spiritual Depths
- Servanthood vs. Servitude
- The Bible
- A Cup of Cold Water
- Celebrating Results
- The Thrill of It All

There is a registration fee of [*$ amount*], which covers the cost of the text, other supplies, and refreshments. Your registration indicates your commitment to attend all sessions.

The course offers a rich mixture of practical theology, psychology, and sociology that will help you live your Christianity fully—to practice it holistically. This course can help you grow in understanding and practice as a caring Christian. Registration forms for those interested are enclosed. We hope to share this experience with you beginning [*month, date*].

[*Typical Closing*],
[*Name*]

....

☐ YES, I am interested in taking part in the course "Christian Caregiving—a Way of Life." Enclosed is $_____.

Name: _____

Address: _____

_____

Phone: _____

Signature: _____

☐ I am interested in taking this course, but cannot do so now. Please let me know the next time the class is offered.

Posters and Signs

Sample Poster 1	**Sample Poster 2**

How
Do
Christians
Care?
Christian Caregiving—
a Way of Life
The skills of Christian
caregiving explored and
practiced.
[*day of week*] [*time*]
[*date to date*]
[*place*]
Call: [*name or place*] [*number*]
for more information

Caring
Christian Caring
Christian Caregiving
Christian Caregiving—a Way of Life
Discover ways
for YOU
to become a
distinctively Christian
caregiver
[*day of week*] [*time*]
[*date to date*]
[*place*]
Call: [*name or place*] [*number*]
for more information

The following are sample outdoor signs (suggested 3' x 5' or 4' x 6' plywood, painted with a simple message in very large, readable letters).

Sample Sign 1	**Sample Sign 2**

Christian
Caring Skills
For Your Life
[*day of week*] [*time*]
[*date to date*]
[*place*]
Call: [*number*]

Christian
Caregiving
Class
[*day of week*] [*time*]
[*date to date*]
[*place*]
Call: [*number*]

Sample Press Release

Course on Christian Caregiving to Be Offered at [*Name of Congregation*]

[*Name of Congregation*] will offer a course called "Christian Caregiving—a Way of Life" beginning in [*month*]. The [*7-week/10-week*] course will explore caring for one another and how it can be uniquely Christian. Participants will practice caring skills and learn how to make distinctively Christian caring and relating a *way of life*.

Led by [*name of leader(s)*] of [*name of congregation*], the course is based on the book *Christian Caregiving—a Way of Life* by Kenneth Haugk, a pastor and clinical psychologist who is the founder of the Stephen Series system of lay caring ministry. Dr. Haugk's book examines the theology, psychology, and practice of distinctively Christian caring. The course at [*name of congregation*] will emphasize the practical application of caring skills to special situations and everyday relationships.

The course includes such topics as:

- God as the Curegiver
- Move Over, Freud!
- Ministering to the Whole Person
- A Surprise Gift: Forgiveness
- Tools of Your Trade: Their Use and Abuse
- Prayer
- Hope-Full Caregiving

Beginning on [*day of week, month/date*], the class will meet every [*day of week*] from [*time*] to [*time*] for seven weeks at [*place*]. We have also scheduled a Friday evening and an all-day Saturday retreat for [*dates*].

or

Beginning on [*day of week, month, date*], the class will meet every [*day of week*] from [*time*] to [*time*] for 10 weeks at [*place where first meeting will be*].

Registration deadline is [*date*]. For further details and registration information call [*name of church*] at [*phone number*].

Sample Radio/TV Public Service Announcement

A [*7-week/10-week*] course called "Christian Caregiving—a Way of Life" will be offered at [*name of congregation*] beginning [*day of week, month, date*]. Learn the skills of caring for one another in a distinctively Christian way. Learn how to share Bible passages, how to pray, how to offer blessings, how to share God's love with others. Learn how to make Christian caregiving part of your everyday life.

Registration deadline is [*date*]. For further information call [*phone number*]. That phone number again is [*phone number*].

Stephen Ministry:
A Lay Caring Ministry for Your Congregation

Thousands of congregations where people have read and studied *Christian Caregiving—a Way of Life* have also enrolled in the Stephen Series.

The Stephen Series (called Stephen Ministry when it's implemented in a congregation) is a complete system for training and organizing laypeople for caring ministry in and around their congregations.

Stephen Ministry enables congregations to recruit, train, and support lay caregivers called Stephen Ministers, who walk alongside a hurting person and offer high-quality, one-to-one, confidential Christian care. Stephen Ministers provide care and support to people experiencing grief, divorce, hospitalization, relocation, chronic or terminal illness, unemployment, loneliness, military mobilization, and countless other life crises or challenges.

More than 12,000 congregations and organizations representing more than 160 denominations from across the United States, Canada, and many other countries have turned to the Stephen Series as a means of multiplying caring ministry.

Visit www.stephenministries.org to learn more about Stephen Ministry. If you have questions or would like to receive a packet of information about how to begin Stephen Ministry in your congregation, call Stephen Ministries at (314) 428-2600.

Books and Courses from Stephen Ministries

Don't Sing Songs to a Heavy Heart:
How to Relate to Those Who Are Suffering

Pastors, lay caregivers, and suffering people alike have high praise for this book by Kenneth Haugk—a warm and practical resource on what to do and say when people are hurting. Forged in the crucible of Dr. Haugk's own suffering and grief, *Don't Sing Songs to a Heavy Heart* draws from his personal experience and from extensive research with more than 4,000 others who have experienced suffering in their lives.

A great follow-up to the *Christian Caregiving—a Way of Life* course, *Don't Sing Songs to a Heavy Heart* offers practical guidance and common-sense suggestions for how to care in ways that hurting people welcome—while avoiding the pitfalls that can add to their suffering. This book combines sound psychology with solid biblical truths to touch caregivers' hearts and help them find the words and actions that will bring God's presence and care to hurting people.

To find more information about *Don't Sing Songs to a Heavy Heart,* read excerpts, or order copies, visit www.stephenministries.org/care. You can also call Stephen Ministries at (314) 428-2600.

Journeying through Grief

A set of four short books that individuals, congregations, and other organizations can share with grieving people at four crucial times during the first year after a loved one has died.

Book 1: *A Time to Grieve,* sent three weeks after the loss

Book 2: *Experiencing Grief,* sent three months after the loss

Book 3: *Finding Hope and Healing,* sent six months after the loss

Book 4: *Rebuilding and Remembering,* sent eleven months after the loss

Each book focuses on the feelings and issues the bereaved person is likely to be experiencing at that point, offering reassurance, encouragement, and hope. In *Journeying through Grief,* Kenneth Haugk writes in a warm, caring style, with short, easy-to-read chapters. He shares from the heart, drawing on his personal and professional experience and from the insights of many others. The books provide a simple yet powerful way to reach out to a grieving person with four caring touches throughout the difficult first year.

Each set comes with four mailing envelopes and a tracking card that makes it easy to know when to send each book.

Also available is a *Giver's Guide* containing suggestions for using the books as well as sample letters that can be personalized and adapted to send with the books.

To find more information about *Journeying through Grief,* read excerpts, or order copies, visit www.stephenministries.org/care. You can also call Stephen Ministries at (314) 428-2600.

Speaking the Truth in Love:
How to Be an Assertive Christian

This book invites the reader to live assertively—just as Jesus did. Building on a scriptural understanding of assertive living, it shows the reader how to develop healthy relationships with others—one to one, in small groups, in task-oriented teams, and in congregations.

This deeply spiritual and extremely practical book makes clear:

- what assertiveness is (and is not)
- the Biblical foundation for assertiveness
- how Jesus is our model for living assertively
- how to be assertive in prayer and praise
- how to make, refuse, and negotiate requests
- how to express and receive compliments
- how to handle criticism, anger, and other tough relational issues

You will learn practical ways to relate to others with greater honesty, compassion, and respect. Experience the freedom and joy of Christian assertiveness!

To find more information about *Speaking the Truth in Love,* read excerpts, or order copies, visit www.stephenministries.org/assertive. You can also call Stephen Ministries at (314) 428-2600.

Discovering God's Vision for Your Life: You and Your Spiritual Gifts

Motivate and mobilize for meaningful ministry

Discovering God's Vision for Your Life is a comprehensive set of resources that congregations can use to build a thriving spiritual gifts ministry.

The centerpiece of these resources is an eight-hour course that helps people discover, understand, and celebrate the gifts God has given to them. During the course, participants:

- learn the biblical foundation of spiritual gifts—how the Holy Spirit has equipped each of them uniquely for ministry
- use the *Haugk Spiritual Gifts Inventory,* developed over six years by a team of social scientists and biblical scholars, to discover which spiritual gifts they have
- identify ways they can put their spiritual gifts into action—ways that get them excited to be involved in ministry

As a result:

- people engage in ministries they're deeply passionate about;
- more and stronger ministry happens in congregations;
- more needs are met inside and outside the church; and
- people are drawn into God's vision—as individuals and as a community of faith.

To find more information about *Discovering God's Vision for Your Life,* read what pastors and lay leaders are saying about this course, or order copies, visit www.stephenministries.org/spiritualgifts. You can also call Stephen Ministries at (314) 428-2600.

Antagonists in the Church: How to Identify and Deal with Destructive Conflict

A ministry-saving resource for pastors and lay leaders

Antagonists are individuals who, on the basis of nonsubstantive evidence, go out of their way to make insatiable demands, usually attacking the person or performance of others. These attacks are selfish in nature, tearing down rather than building up, and are often directed against those in a leadership capacity. (From chapter 2, "What Is Church Antagonism?")

Pastors, church staff, governing boards, lay leaders, and others will find the insights, principles, and practical methods offered by this book valuable for identifying and dealing with individuals who attack leaders and destroy ministry—as well as for creating a congregation environment that prevents future attacks.

The *Study Guide* turns the book into a course to equip a group of church leaders to effectively deal with and prevent antagonistic attacks. It includes discussion questions for each chapter, which help course participants apply the strategies and concepts to their own unique situations.

To find more information about *Antagonists in the Church,* read excerpts, watch a video featuring firsthand accounts by five pastors who learned how to deal with antagonists through this book, or order copies of the book and *Study Guide,* visit www.stephenministries.org/antagonists. You can also call Stephen Ministries at (314) 428-2600.

Me, an Evangelist? Every Christian's Guide to Caring Evangelism

This down-to-earth book presents an engaging story about a reluctant evangelist while exploring the principles and practices of sharing our faith in daily life. Author William J. McKay teaches Christians how to express God's Good News in ways that others welcome. Biblical and practical, this book shows how to joyfully, comfortably, and naturally live and share the love of Jesus with others.

Caring Evangelism: How to Live and Share Christ's Love

Evangelism training for people who never thought they could be evangelists

This course turns the book *Me, an Evangelist?* into a learning experience designed to help Christians share their faith with others naturally and comfortably. As participants grow spiritually, they are equipped to show Christ's love in their daily lives by words and actions that others appreciate. This course can provide a strong foundation for your congregation's spiritual growth, evangelism, and outreach efforts.

You can order *Me, an Evangelist?* or *Caring Evangelism* course resources by visiting www.stephenministries.org or calling (314) 428-2600.

Reopening the Back Door: Answers to Questions about Ministering to Inactive Members

Written in a unique question-and-answer format, this book offers practical guidance for how to reach out to people when their commitment to their faith community has diminished. Author Kenneth Haugk explains what most often leads people to withdraw from the church, what words and behaviors drive people even farther away, how to prevent inactivity, and how to welcome inactive members back home.

Caring for Inactive Members: How to Make God's House a Home

A caring approach to a sensitive situation

This six-hour course takes the anxiety out of ministering to inactive members by equipping participants to relate confidently and effectively to those who are separated or alienated from the church community. Church staff, lay leaders, and congregation members can use these resources to address the issues that can cause inactivity, to care for inactive members, and to invite them back into God's house.

You can order *Reopening the Back Door* or *Caring for Inactive Members* course resources by visiting www.stephenministries.org or calling (314) 428-2600.

The following four books are Stephen Ministries Care Classics®—highly esteemed books on Christian caring and relating that were previously out of print. Stephen Ministries has republished them as Care Classics for the benefit of this and future generations. You can order these books by visiting www.stephenministries.org or calling (314) 428-2600.

The Promise of Hope: Coping When Life Caves In
by William M. Kinnaird

A personal witness of faith and courage. Bill Kinnaird brings a message of hope to those who struggle and suffer. Amid the turmoil of daily life, he offers a place filled with reason, purpose, and the reassurance that God is always there.

Joy Comes with the Morning: The Positive Power of Christian Encouragement
by William M. Kinnaird

A wealth of personal insights and timeless ideas for Christian caregiving. Whether for daily meditations or study by a group, this book helps readers experience God's love for and through God's people.

Yes, Lord

by Dona Hoffman

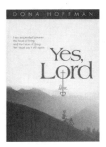

Poems, journal entries, and correspondence chart the journey of Dona Hoffman through the struggles that follow her diagnosis of terminal cancer. Dona's courage, love, faith, and humor will charm and encourage both those who suffer and those who care for others.

Caring Criticism: Building Bridges Instead of Walls

by William J. Diehm

This book meets a challenging topic head on: giving and receiving criticism. Combining Christian love and Biblical principles, pastor and psychologist William Diehm shares practical, down-to-earth advice on how to offer criticism in ways that are helpful and non-threatening, how to receive criticism without taking offense or feeling crushed, and how to respond positively to criticism.

APPENDIX D

Stephen Ministries St. Louis

Stephen Ministries is a not-for-profit Christian education and publishing organization founded in 1975 and based in St. Louis, Missouri. Its mission is:

> To equip the saints for the work of ministry, for building up the body of Christ, until all of us come to the unity of the faith and of the knowledge of the Son of God, to maturity, to the measure of the full stature of Christ.
>
> *Ephesians 4:12–13*

Stephen Ministries' 40-person staff develops and delivers high-quality, Christ-centered training and resources to:

- help congregations and other organizations equip and organize people to do meaningful ministry; and

- help individuals grow spiritually, relate and care more effectively, and live out their faith in daily life.

Stephen Ministries is best known for Stephen Ministry—a lay caring ministry for congregations. As a publisher, it also offers resources in other areas, including grief support, assertiveness, ministry mobilization, caring evangelism, church antagonism, spiritual formation, leadership, inactive member ministry, and spiritual gifts.

To learn more or to order resources, contact us at:

Stephen Ministries
2045 Innerbelt Business Center Drive
St. Louis, Missouri 63114-5765
(314) 428-2600
www.stephenministries.org

ABOUT THE AUTHORS

Rev. Kenneth C. Haugk, Ph.D., a pastor and clinical psychologist, is the founder and Executive Director of Stephen Ministries St. Louis (www. stephenministries.org), best known for the Stephen Series system of lay caring ministry. Dr. Haugk is involved in the day-to-day leadership of Stephen Ministries and in developing new leaders throughout the organization. He has written numerous books and courses and regularly speaks at conferences on such subjects as Christian caregiving, grief, inactive member ministry, church and business antagonism, leadership, and spiritual gifts.

William J. McKay, M.Div., served as a pastor in Boulder, Colorado, before coming to Stephen Ministries St. Louis. As Director of Project Development, he has led Stephen Ministries' program team in developing a wide range of ministry resources, including the complete rewrite of the *Stephen Ministry Leader's Manual,* and is continuing to lead the development of new projects to support ministry. Rev. McKay is a member of the teaching faculty at Stephen Series Leader's Training Courses.

IT WAS A BLESSING TO DECLINE TO
MOVE WITH BILL UPON HIS JOB OFFER

BEING A PARISHONER AT ST
THOMAS AND HAVING THE
FAMILY I HAVE HERE IN GA.

———·———·———·———·———

MAY GOD BLESS AND PROTECT
BOTH OF YOU IN ~~THEIR~~ YOUR DAILY
LIVING AND KEEP ~~THEM~~ YOU SAFE
IN ~~GOD'S~~ HIS LOVING HANDS. GIVE MAY HE
~~THEM~~ YOU THE STRENGTH AND COURAGE
TO BE FAITHFUL IN ALL THAT
~~THEY~~ YOU MAY ENCOUNTER AND
TRUST IN WHAT MAY BE GIVEN
TO ~~THEM~~ YOU THROUGH CHRIST
OUR LORD.